# BEAUTIFUL BALI

*By the same author*
Monash University: the First Ten Years.

# BEAUTIFUL
# BALI

★

## Sir Robert Blackwood

★

HAMPDEN HALL

MELBOURNE

*First published 1970*

© Text, illustrations and map copyright
of Sir Robert Blackwood

*Registered in Australia for transmission by post as a book*
Published by Hampden Hall,
P.O. Box 30, Victoria 3186, Australia.

Text entirely set and printed in Australia by
Halstead Press, Sydney,
on paper produced in Australia by Associated Pulp and
Paper Manufacturers Ltd., Burnie, Tasmania.

National Library of Australia
Card Service Number and Standard Book Number
SBN 909908 00 1

# Contents

# Illustrations

## TEXT FIGURES

# *Foreword*

On my first visit to the island of Bali I was singularly fortunate in becoming acquainted with my friends Djati and Janice Mantjika, the proprietors of Jan's Tours and Travel Service in Denpasar. I owe a debt of gratitude to these people for introducing me to the island and its inhabitants and for their guidance in acquiring a knowledge of the life and customs of the Balinese. Without their assistance that first visit would have been comparatively meaningless although intensely interesting as a spectacle. For, much to my surprise, no informative guide book was available to the tourist. Nor could the visitor obtain a map of the island which would reveal its physical features and show the location of the chief points of interest together with the road system serving them.

Before visiting the island for a second time I studied all the literature available covering its past history, its religious inheritance, its social customs and its artistic achievements. In particular I am indebted to Miguel Covarrubias, whose book *Island of Bali* published in 1937 is a tremendous source of information on these aspects of Balinese life. Although there have been many changes since the date of its publication, this book gave me a much greater understanding of many of the things I saw on my first visit and of many more which I have seen on subsequent visits to the island.

In order to remedy a deficiency which clearly exists, I have seen fit to produce this handbook which I have written specifically and unashamedly for the use of the tourist. It is designed to introduce him to the island, its history, its people, their way of life, their art forms and their achievements. Enough basic information on these subjects is included to enable the visitor to appreciate the things he sees and to understand the many facets of Balinese life he will observe going on around him. Additionally I have included enough information about the particular places he will visit during a short stay on the island to ensure his intelligent appreciation of them.

At the same time the text and the illustrations have been designed to provide a readable, although somewhat condensed account of the island and its people, which will appeal to the general reader as being interesting and informative in itself even in the absence of an actual visit.

If this handbook enables the visitor to Bali to get as much enjoyment and interest out of his contact with it as I myself have done, my efforts will have been well repaid.

ROBERT BLACKWOOD
Melbourne, Australia

December, 1969

# 1

# The Island

The island of Bali lies immediately to the east of Java from which it is separated by the comparatively shallow Bali Strait which is only some two miles across. It extends in an east-west direction for ninety-five miles, lying between longitude 114° 25′ East and longitude 115° 43′ East. In a north-south direction it extends for fifty miles between latitude 8° 03′ South and latitude 8° 51′ South. The island is not a large one, having an area of only 2,147 square miles, but what it lacks in size is more than compensated for by the grandeur of its mountainous terrain, its extreme fertility, its endless beauty, and the artistry and charm of its people.

The greater part of the island is mountainous and like Java itself, and the majority of the Lesser Sunda Islands, is of volcanic origin. The western section of the island is a long narrow promontory and is an arid, almost uninhabited upland which rises to some 4,000 feet above sea level. Covered with scrub and low forest it provides cover for deer and wild pig which are frequently seen. Formerly tigers were also known to inhabit this section of the island, but they are now very rarely encountered. The western uplands lead to the forested central highlands which culminate in the volcanic peaks of Mt. Batukau at an elevation of 7,707 feet and Mt. Tjatur at an elevation of 7,013 feet. On the mountains are three lakes of great beauty, deep set and surrounded by thick tropical forest. These are Lakes Bratan, Bujan and Tambelangan. The central highlands are separated from the eastern highlands by a saddle between them, but still at an elevation of 4,000 feet. The eastern highlands, also volcanic in origin, culminate in the majestic volcanic cone of Mt. Agung or Bali Peak, at an elevation of 10,308 feet. Mt. Agung erupted early in 1963 causing a considerable amount of death and destruction amongst the villages on its southern slopes. To the north-west of Mt. Agung is the subsidiary peak of Mt. Abang (7,058 feet) and at the foot of this mountain lies a caldera some seven miles across and 1,500 feet deep. This caldera contains within the confines of its almost circular rim, the crater lake Batur (Plate 1) and the still active volcanic peak of Mt. Batur rising to 5,633 feet. Mt. Batur erupted in 1917 with the loss of thousands of homes and very many lives. The lava engulfed the ancient village of Batur on the western edge of the lake, but stopped short at the very gate of the village temple. Taking this as a favourable sign the villagers continued to live there, only to see the site completely buried under a lava flow following a subsequent eruption in 1926. Crater villages are now confined to the eastern edge of the lake remote from the volcano, which still emits small amounts of steam and vapour forty-three years later.

North of the highlands lies a narrow coastal lowland fringe of occupied and arable land. The coastline is unbroken, affording no shelter. During the northwest monsoon season the roadstead at Buleleng, the port of the former capital, Singaradja, becomes unsafe for shipping. Only a small proportion of the population of Bali live on the northern lowlands, which are comparatively dry and hot. The vast bulk of the population inhabits the very much larger area of lowland to the south of the central and eastern highlands. Here the climate is cooler and the rainfall greater. The southern lowland is dissected by many streams and rivers which rise high up on the mountain slopes and have cut deeply into the soft volcanic rock. Steep sided and narrow, terraced for rice growing, green and verdant, these river valleys are of great beauty (Plate 2). The rivers are in the main fast-flowing shallow streams which are not navigable. They are subject to marked variations of flow occasioned by short term localised variations in rainfall, and in the wet season from November to May, flash floods are frequent and dangerous. They do, however, provide a regular supply of water to feed the well-developed irrigation system which has been built up over the centuries by the Balinese to irrigate the extraordinarily extensive and well-developed network of rice terraces. Every available piece of land which can be used for rice growing is terraced and in places the terraces extend from the bottoms of the valleys right to the summits of adjacent mountain ranges. In the southern lowlands the population density exceeds 1,500 persons per square mile, but such is the intensity of rice cultivation that the island continues to be self-sufficient in rice production.

At the extreme south of the island is a tableland rising to an elevation of 700 feet, formerly known to the Dutch as the Tafelhoek, but now known to the Balinese as the Bukit. Unlike the main body of the island this area is not volcanic in origin but is a deposit of marine limestone rising, for the most part, sheer from the sea in cliffs up to 250 feet in height. On one of these at the extreme southwest stands the impressive temple of Uluwatu, a spectacular sentinel overlooking the Indian Ocean. This tableland is connected to the main island by a narrow isthmus on which the airport for Denpasar is located at Tuban. This isthmus in association with a narrow spur extending northeasterly from the Bukit, forms the only sheltered harbour on the island at Benoa, the port of Denpasar. The port is only accessible to small ships however, since the entrance through the fringing coral reef is both narrow and tortuous.

To the southeast of Bali lies the small island of Nusa Penida, an arid marine limestone tableland similar in every respect to the Bukit.

The flora and fauna of Bali are typically Javanese and typically tropical. The forests are composed of many species of trees, predominant among which is the coral tree or *dap dap (Erythrina lithosperma)* easily recognised by its tall open structure, its light sage-green foliage and its masses of small bright red flowers. It is not a tree of commercial importance as far as its wood is concerned, but it is widely used as a shade tree for coffee and other crops and as a source of wood fuel. Teak *(djati)* is present, but sparsely so. The main sources of first grade timbers for structural work are *kuanditan (Aglaia odoratissima)*, *ketangi (Lagerstroemia speciosa)*, *kepelan (Manglietia glauca)* and *djuwet (Crypteronia paniculata)*. Species of *Podocarpus* and *Casuarina* are prolific in their occurrence and the visitor will observe stands of pines *(Pinus mercusi)* around the crater rim of Lake Batur. The *pala* (*Dipterocarpus haseltii*) is a tall straight tree rising to a height of some 200 feet, a very good stand of which forms the monkey forest at Sangeh. Various varieties of mahogany are present.

Important amongst the many species of palm are the coconut palm, which supplies cooking oil and copra; the Palmyra or *lontar* palm, the dried leaves of which were formerly used for making books and which are now used for making *lamaks* for festival decorations (Plate 35); the sago palm whose sap makes toddy and whose fibre (*idjuk*) makes thatch; and the thorny *salak* palm which produces a pleasantly flavoured nut. Many tropical fruits, such as papaya, mangosteen, rambutan, bananas, durien and jackfruit are grown, while flowering frangipanni and hibiscus bushes abound and orchids are common. The banyan tree, or *waringin*, is conspicuous in many village centres and is held sacred by the Balinese as also is the *kepuh* tree, very often found growing in cemeteries and temple precincts.

Deer and wild pig are numerous and damage crops. Tigers are present in the western uplands but are very rarely seen. Likewise crocodiles which could formerly be seen in the Prantjak river are now rarely encountered. Wild buffalo are not found, and indeed the farm water buffalo is infrequently seen in southern Bali. Ploughing and preparation of the rice terraces is done mainly with cattle, a local breed with soft orange-brown pelts, always immaculately groomed. Wild monkeys are prevalent in the forests.

The population of the island is now estimated at approximately 2.3 million people (1969). The capital of the island and present seat of government is Denpasar in the south. Singaradja on the north coast was the former capital and seat of government under the Dutch. Gilimanuk on the west is the terminal of the ferry from Ketapang on the island of Java. Other important towns in the south are Gianjar, Klungkung, Karangasem and Tabanan. All these towns are linked by a coastal road which extends right round the island, while there are three main routes connecting the southern lowlands with the north coast lowlands. In addition there are many local roads in the southern lowlands. Some of these roads are rough and unpaved, some are fit only for four-wheel-drive vehicles, but in the main most of the important roads, some 500 miles in all, are sealed roads of reasonably good standard.

The weather in Bali is always warm and humid, but the heat is tempered by sea breezes and cool air from the mountains. There are no hot and cold seasons, the maximum daily temperature approximating 85°F. in the south and 90°F. in the north. There are, however, distinct wet and dry seasons. The dry season extends from May to November when the southeast monsoon prevails and the rainfall is low. This is the best time to visit the island. The wet season extends from November to May, when the northwest monsoon prevails and rainfall is high and often violent. The average annual rainfall at Singaradja in the north is 45 inches. At Denpasar in the south it is 90 inches.

The mountains are regarded by the Balinese as holy, as the home of the gods and as the source of well-being and fertility. The Gunung Agung (Mt. Agung) is regarded as the navel of the world, as the home of Siwa and other important gods. To the Balinese it stands in the same relation as Kailasa and Meru do to the Hindus of India. On the other hand the sea, which is lower even than the land, represents everything evil to the Balinese, a view reinforced by the presence in it of harmful and unpleasant creatures such as sharks, sea snakes and various poisonous fish. In consequence the Balinese have little maritime tendency and look to the land and to the mountain rather than to the sea for their support and well-being. Bali is regarded as the entire world, floating in the ocean, supported by the mythical turtle and entwined snakes, a combination which appears in many rituals, sculptures and shrines.

At the back of this book an authentic map of the island of Bali will be found. It has been specially compiled using as a basis the navigation maps of the island and an old Dutch map produced in 1935 which is no longer available. Excessive detail has been avoided in the interest of clarity, but sufficient information has been included to enable the visitor to Bali to study the features of the island and to locate the main points of interest described in Part Two of this book, which he will want to see.

# 2

# *The History of Bali*

It is certain that man has been present in the Indonesian islands for a very long time. Fossils of 'Java man' were first found in Java by Eugene Dubois in the 1890's. These were later identified as *Homo erectus* now definitely recognised as an early species of man in existence from 400,000 to 800,000 years ago. Later discoveries on the Solo River at Trinul brought to light the remains of 'Solo man', an early form of *Homo sapiens* who appeared on the scene some 100,000 years ago and continued in existence until about 40,000 years ago. Between the fossil record and the historical record however, there is a considerable gap in our knowledge of the history of man in Indonesia, little factual evidence being available until the fifth century A.D.

Early Indonesians are thought to have been of Negrito character, modified by immigration from southern China about 2,000 B.C. These people were known broadly as Proto-Malays, and in fact our earliest records concerning the area are derived from Chinese writings. Notwithstanding their primitive character, they nevertheless developed a social structure, village life, rice culture, animal husbandry and fishing. Their religious beliefs were animistic based on the concept that all objects, animate and inanimate, are possessed of a spirit or soul. The spirits formed the basis of worship, good and favourable spirits being patronised and the evil ones being placated with offerings. In those days many natural phenomena were explicable only on a supernatural basis. Priests were those whose minds were powerful enough to control or influence others. These animistic beliefs are an important feature of Balinese life to this day.

---

PLATE 1. Caldera of Mt. Batur with Lake Batur as seen looking east from Penelokan.

PLATE 2. Rice terraces on the banks of the River Petanu.

6

Early in the Christian era, probably about 200 A.D., the countries of southeast Asia came under the influence of Hindu culture as a result of trade from India extending through the Straits of Malacca to Sumatra and Java. The traders were followed by Brahmin priests who converted the ruling chieftains to the worship of Hindu gods. The influence of Hinduism was strong and continued for several centuries, although still allied to animistic beliefs and practices. Indian influence inculcated the caste system into Indonesia and later introduced the Buddhist religion. It was responsible for the introduction of the concept of the godliness of royalty and the ruling classes, the use of Sanskrit as the language of religion and the aristocracy, and the introduction of Indian mythology—the stories of the Mahabrata and the Ramayana. These latter have been modified to suit the Indonesian character and form the basis of most of the folklore, drama, dancing and art forms of the Balinese at the present time.

By the sixth century A.D. Sumatra and Java were under strong Buddhist influence. It is clear however, that this had not displaced Hinduism, but was contemporary with it. Sea trade through the Straits of Malacca between India and China was responsible for the rapid devolopment of a maritime empire in south Sumatra known as Srividjaya, whose existence depended on the possession of export commodities and control of the sea routes of the region. Java became a basic agricultural civilisation based on its extensive and richly productive irrigated rice lands, and was controlled by a succession of kingdoms commencing with the Mataram and concluding with the Madjapahit kingdom. Between Srividjaya and Madjapahit there was continuing rivalry, a basic antagonism which has had its influence even since the declaration of Indonesian independence in 1945.

The early Javanese kingdoms have left some of the most magnificent archaeological remains as testimony of their greatness. In central Java near Jogjakarta, one of the most impressive Buddhist monuments in existence today still

---

PLATE 3. Selling Bona baskets and ivory carvings at Bedulu.

PLATE 4. Girls carrying temple offerings.

B

stands. It is the vast temple of Borobudur, built early in the ninth century. This was for centuries hidden under a heavy layer of volcanic ash and so escaped Muslim depredation. It was excavated and restored early this century by the Dutch. The power of the central Javanese kingdoms, of which Borobudur is the epitome, seems to have declined by the end of the tenth century and passed to east Java to the kingdom of Madjapahit. After the thirteenth century Srividjaya declined in power and Madjapahit became dominant in the whole region. Madjapahit prospered greatly and at its height controlled for the first time in history, almost the whole of present day Indonesia as well as the larger part of the Malay peninsula. However, its decline began in the latter part of the fourteenth century. It declined still further when the rise of Malacca, a centre of Islam, deprived it of maritime control of the main trade routes. The rivalry between the Hindu state of Madjapahit and Islam continued until the collapse of the Madjapahit kingdom at the end of the fifteenth century, when Islam became dominant in Sumatra and Java.

As Islam spread in Java, Hindu-Buddhist priests together with the aristocracy, scholars, savants, artists and their followers, took refuge in Bali and western Lombok, taking with them the material culture of Madjapahit, including books which have since revealed some of the splendours of that kingdom.

In 1511 the Portuguese captured Malacca and the consolidation of their trade route from Goa to Macao and the development of their trade with the spice islands helped Islam to progress eastwards during the sixteenth century.

The sixteenth to the eighteenth centuries saw the penetration of European influence into the area of southeast Asia. This was motivated primarily by the demand for spices on the European markets, centred in Venice. In those days spices were used not merely to flavour food, but to preserve it. This was particularly so in the case of meat which decomposes quickly in tropical climates and to a considerable extent even in European climates. The spice trade attracted the Portuguese in the first place, but they were quickly followed by the English, Dutch, Spanish and French. The Portuguese influence never grew beyond the maintenance of a string of trade bases along the main eastern sea route, but the British ultimately became involved in government and administration as well as in trade in India and Malaya, the Spanish in the Philippines, the French in Indo-China and the Dutch in Indonesia.

From a precarious beginning in 1596 the Dutch gradually extended their control of Indonesia, which they governed, if somewhat uneasily, for almost 350 years. Early in the seventeenth century they set up their headquarters in Jakatra, which they renamed Batavia. By the end of the seventeenth century they were fully in control of a country which had become weakened after the decline of the Madjapahit influence. During the eighteenth century Dutch power itself declined due to a collapse of the spice trade, and early in the nineteenth century the Napoleonic wars nearly ended Dutch rule in Indonesia. The British took over control of Java from 1810 until the end of the Napoleonic wars. During this period the Dutch export trade was lost to Britain, but on their return to Java in 1824 they began to produce large export crops sold through Amsterdam, which became a powerful centre of European trade in coffee, tea, tobacco, pepper, sugar and cotton. These were produced at the expense of rice, but the revenue derived from them helped to provide the country with roads and railways. Consequent impoverishment of the country, the harshness of Dutch rule and the denial of any share of government to the Indonesians, embittered them against 'colonial control' and led to the great movement towards independent nationalism which was latent but real when Japan entered the second world war in 1941. Events moved so fast that what had taken the colonial powers four hundred years to achieve was lost in four months. The Japanese conquest of Singapore and Malaya, Burma, Indonesia and the Philippines was complete by April 1942.

In Indonesia, the Japanese, although maintaining military control of the country, appointed a government under the leadership of Soekarno and Hatta nominally to administer the country. These two leaders of the independence movement used every opportunity to advance that cause, and when the war in the East was concluded with the surrender of the Japanese on 10 August, 1945, Soekarno and Hatta declared the independence of Indonesia by proclamation in Jakarta on 17 August, 1945. When the British and later the Dutch came to take over from the Japanese they were presented with a *fait accompli*, but at once set about the task of restoring the pre-war *status quo*. However, Indonesian resistance was such that the Dutch were finally forced, in the face of world opinion, to grant 'unconditional and irrevocable' independence to the Indonesian Republic on 27 December, 1949.

Soekarno was proclaimed the first President of the Republic. A man with a dynamic public image, he endeavoured to run the Republic as a 'guided democracy' always seeking political solutions to the many problems and ignoring the economic reconstruction necessary to lift the country out of the impoverished state it had fallen into by being cut off from international trade during the war. The economic situation deteriorated still further as severe inflation set in, until finally on 1 October, 1965 a communist effort to overthrow the army command and take over the country proved unsuccessful. General Suharto, head of the army's strategic reserve, took strong counter action and by the same evening was in control of the situation. Soekarno was clearly seen to be in sympathy with the abortive coup, and was replaced as President by Suharto, although this was not proclaimed officially until some two years after Soekarno was stripped of his powers. Since that time the government of Suharto has made strenuous efforts to correct the Republic's economic difficulties, and present indications are that a reasonable degree of stability has been achieved.

The history of Bali itself is obscure until the beginning of the eleventh century, but since that time it has been bound up with that of Java in the first place and the Indonesian Republic in the second. In 991 A.D. a prince named Erlangga was born of a Balinese king and a Javanese princess. He later went to Java, married a princess from Srividjaya, and succeeded to the throne of Kahuripan, one of the kingdoms of central Java, which he ruled for thirty years while his brother, Anak Wungsu, ruled in Bali in his name. Thus a link was forged between Java and Bali at that time and

Erlangga became one of the most famous of Balinese mythical figures.

Later Bali became independent of Java but was again subjugated by the king of Singasari in 1284. When Singasari was absorbed into the Madjapahit dynasty, Bali again became free only to return to the vassaldom of Madjapahit in 1343. The Balinese continued to revolt against their subordination to Madjapahit, but these revolts were put down, the final defeat being by Gadja Mada the supreme general and prime minister of Madjapahit, to whom the Balinese aristocracy ascribes its origin.

With the advance of Islam and the decline and final destruction of the empire of Madjapahit early in the sixteenth century, Bali as its remaining dependence, became the refuge of the Prince and his court, the priests, artists and scholars of Madjapahit. The Prince proclaimed himself King of Bali and Radja of Klungkung. He it was who divided the island into eight principalities which he gave to his relatives and generals to govern. These later became the smaller kingdoms of Badung, Tabanan, Bangli, Gianjar, Klungkung, Karangasem, Buleleng and Djembrana, each with its own Radja, into which Bali became divided and which today are still divisions for local government.

This movement was of immense significance to the development of Bali. The grafting of the culture of the cream of the intellectuals of the most civilised people of the East Indies to the simple animism of the Balinese has produced one of the most colourful, interesting and artistic civilisations that could be encountered. The art and the philosophy of the Hindu-Javanese have been preserved in the art and philosophy of the Hindu-Balinese, and have indeed flourished in that atmosphere.

The Dutch first visited the island of Bali by ship in 1597 and were enchanted with the island. Their reports in Holland on their return attracted Dutch traders and the Dutch East India Company to the island in succeeding years. The Balinese princes were friendly but remained aloof. While recognising the authority of the Dutch, they retained their own individual autonomy in their own principalities. In 1846, however, the Dutch sent a military expedition to

North Bali following the plundering of wrecks by the Balinese, and finally took over the states of Buleleng and Djembrana in 1882. In 1894 the Dutch drove the Balinese out of the island of Lombok after military action. This was followed by dissension amongst the Radjas of Bali. The States of Badung, Klungkung and Bangli made common cause against Gianjar. The Tjokorde of Ubud persuaded the Radja of Gianjar to ask the Dutch government for help. This was immediately given by the Dutch, who promptly annexed Gianjar in 1900. In 1904 a small Chinese steamer was wrecked at Sanur and was looted by the Balinese. The owners demanded restitution from the Dutch government. Officials were sent to the Radja of Badung to obtain compensation, but this was refused. This incident led to the final struggle between the Radjas of Bali and the Dutch. After the fall of Denpasar, Pemetjutan and finally Klungkung, the struggle ended in 1908 with the Dutch in complete control of the island.

The army remained in authority in Bali until 1914 when it was withdrawn and replaced by police. The former principalities were retained as districts of local government and the Radjas were allowed to rule subject to Dutch supervision and authority.

The overall Dutch administration was centred in Singaradja and remained there until the seat of government was transferred to Denpasar in 1959. The subsequent history of Bali is that of the Republic of Indonesia. The Japanese occupation caused little disruption on the island other than to cut it off from imports, particularly of cotton goods and clothing, and to deplete the rice supply to such an extent that the Balinese suffered real privation. The island suffered more from a lack of control than from suppression. The felling of timber on the highlands, for instance, was allowed to proceed unchecked. This resulted in severe forest denudation which had an adverse effect on run-off from the forests. This in turn depleted the regularity of water supply for rice irrigation, a situation that is still subject to correction.

Most of the Balinese, although initially suspicious of the government set up after the Japanese occupation, were pro-Soekarno because of his part-Balinese origin. However, as a whole they remain politically indifferent, preferring to judge the government by the effect of its actions on their daily lives, on food supply, on price levels and on the general stability of the currency and on economic prosperity. In this regard the government of Suharto finds greater favour.

# 3

# *Village Life and Organisation*

The village life of the people of Bali both moulds their character and reflects their character. The very spirit of Bali emanates from the thousands of village communities that have been established in the main on the fertile southern lowlands. Some of the villages located in the highlands are the homes of the Bali Aga, the original animistic inhabitants, and here in walled villages such as those around Lake Batur and those on the southern slopes of Mt. Agung, such as Tenganan, old customs still prevail. But the vast bulk of the villages follow, with minor variations, a standard pattern of establishment and a standard pattern of government.

Situated amongst the open rice terraces the villages are located in patches of tropical vegetation, where the trees provide not only shady and cool conditions, but also many of the daily needs of the people, such as food, fuel and building materials. Amongst the inevitable coconut palms grow papayas and bananas, breadfruit and mangoes, jackfruit, pomeloes and other tropical fruits. The dark green canopy sheltering each village provides a delightful foil to the emerald green and yellow ochre of the rice fields.

The village is always built along each side of a main roadway which usually runs north and south in the Balinese sense. That is, its direction runs from the mountain (north) towards the sea (south). Lining each side of the road are substantially continuous mud walls protected from the weather by rice straw or woven coconut-palm-leaf thatch (Plate 8). Behind these walls are individual family compounds, each surrounded by its own wall, consisting of a number of small buildings each equivalent to a single room. A gateway through the main village wall gives access to each family compound. Each gateway is entered over a raised doorstep of stone. Each gate along the village wall is the same or at least similar in design, usually a covered entrance surmounted by thatch. Beyond the family compounds access may be had to the unirrigated fruit and vegetable gardens where village requirements of sweet potato, greens, egg plant, maize and sugar cane may be grown.

There are usually a few crossroads in the form of narrow lanes giving access to adjacent rice terraces. At the crossroads in the centre of the village are the important communal facilities, which are often arranged around an open square, an area of magical importance to the Balinese villagers.

Reference to Fig. 1 will give the reader a general picture of a typical Balinese village. Here the essential community centre comprises the village temple, the *pura desa* (A), the hall of assembly, the *balé agung* (B), the arena where cockfights are held, called the *wantilan* (C), the market (D), the village 'bells' or *kulkul* hanging in a tower (E), and in most cases a banyan tree or *waringin* (F), the sacred tree of the Hindus, the shade of which is generally appreciated by the villagers attending meetings or the market.

Very often an open channel carrying water, which may be a part of the local irrigation system, runs down each side of the village's main street and provides for the needs of the villagers. Compounds are then reached by bamboo or stone bridges over these channels. The channels are very often used for bathing, but in any case there will always be public

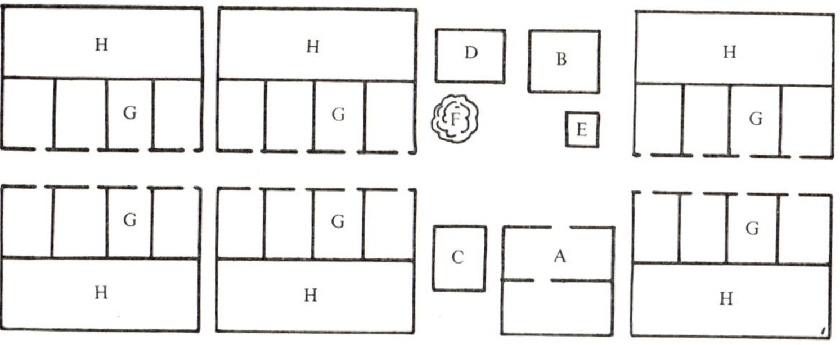

1. Typical arrangement of a Balinese village. A, *Pura desa*, the village temple. B, *Balé agung*, the assembly hall. C, *Wantilan*, the arena. D, Market. E, *Kulkul* tower. F, *Waringin*, sacred banyan tree. G, Family compounds. H, Fruit gardens.

baths nearby, either in an adjacent stream or irrigation channel or in the form of formal baths with water spouting from carved stone figures. On the outskirts of the village there is always a cemetery area. This is usually a rough, unkempt piece of woodland used for temporary burial of the dead pending cremation. Cremation ceremonies are normally held in the cemetery, and there is always a small temple, the *pura dalem* or temple of the dead, located in the cemetery grounds and usually associated with a sacred *kepuh* tree.

Balinese life is adjusted to the climate. Activity commences at first light, generally with bathing, and in the very early morning hours around 4.30 a.m. villagers may be seen going to work in the fields or perhaps to the market. Women will be seen walking to market with their wares on their heads, figures erect and graceful. They will be carrying heavy loads of clay pottery, fruit, vegetables, mats, baskets and so on, even at times carrying on their heads the very table that will be used to display the produce. Later in the day workers will be seen returning from the fields carrying sheaves of rice, the men on bamboo poles slung over their shoulders, the women on their heads. At midday the activity declines due to the heat of the sun, but in the late afternoon it recovers and it is at this time that many colourful village processions may be seen. These are usually connected with temple festivals, or 'birthdays', when the women prepare astonishing displays of food and fruit arranged on elaborate wooden trays. These are carried by them on their heads (Plate 4) as they walk in procession to the temple dressed in gaily coloured garments.

In every village children predominate. Most of them naked, they play around the gates of the family compounds in happy abandon. The fighting cocks, kept by many families, are displayed on the streets in bamboo baskets, through the bottoms of which they can forage amongst the grass or scratch amongst the dirt. The roads are infested with the village dogs. White, mangy and unattractive, they receive little attention from the villagers and are tolerated only as scavengers and for their ability to frighten away evil spirits and intruders by incessant barking at night.

Ducks are carefully herded by boys or elderly people and

are driven to the rice fields daily, using a long bamboo pole topped with white cloth or feathers. At the rice field this pole, planted in the ground, acts as a marker from which the ducks will not stray in their feeding and at which they assemble at sundown for return to the village (Plate 9). The herding of ducks can be seen along the roadside at any time and visitors will observe the ducks feeding unattended around their marker poles in the rice fields. Pigs of a variety little removed from the wild hog are kept tethered within the family compound as a rule, or if kept loose are prevented from wandering by bamboo barricades placed in the gateways. These are not always effective, however, and pigs will be seen quite frequently wandering in the village streets. Black, with long snouts and sagging bellies, they are transported to market trussed and packed in bamboo basketry cages. Chickens generally wander in the family compound and on the roadway where they are frequently killed by passing motor vehicles. For the peace of mind of visitors it should be pointed out that to run over a chicken or any other animal on the road is no crime in Bali. In fact the Balinese compete to recover the corpse as a source of food.

Every Balinese village is a self-contained community in its own right, ruled by a village council, the *krama desa*, which is representative of the villagers as a whole. Every normal married man who has a house or owns a plot of land in the village precincts must be a member of the village association. Refusal to join would result in expulsion from the village society. To be expelled from a village is perhaps the greatest form of punishment by social ostracism. In fact to be disciplined and deprived of any social rights within the village is a punishment far more severe and far more effective than imprisonment. The village social structure is thus used to maintain discipline and punish the evildoer.

Formerly the *krama desa* administered the land of the village, the homes, the communal rice fields, the gardens and the lands for growing bamboo, timber and fuel. Land was at that time the common property of the villages and was allotted only to worthy members of each village for their use purely as tenants. Such communal ownership still applies in the village of Tenganan described in detail later, but of recent years land ownership by individuals has become the rule.

The council usually elects one of its members, a popular and influential man or the son of a former well-respected chief, to be the village head man, or *klian desa*. His services are not paid for, and once elected he cannot refuse office. However he is generally relieved to some small extent from taxes, which provides some slight reward. He presides over meetings, administers the society of the village and organises village festivals.

The village *kulkul*, consisting generally of two hollow wooden logs with on open slot cut in one side of each suspended from an overhead structure on a tower located at the village centre, is used to call the *krama desa* together (Plate 6). By striking the logs with a wooden bar in different positions, high or low notes may be sounded. Patterns of sound combined with patterns of rhythm serve to call the villagers together for various purposes, to sound an alarm, to inform the villagers of processions and other events, and so on. These bell towers are often very ornate in character, ornamented with intricate and elaborate sculpture, with porcelain plates or other added features. They provide a study in themselves of the development of a typical Balinese art form. They are very often incorporated as part of the village temple compound.

When the *krama desa* is called together it meets in the *balé agung*, the village meeting house, generally an open thatched pavilion located at the village centre. Strict precedence governs the order of seating of the members and the newly-elected are generally seated on the floor until the death of some older member creates a vacant seat, from which the member will move as his seniority increases. The *desa* in session makes all the decisions concerning the functioning of the village and the allocation of village duties. It attends to the organisation of festivals and to the welfare of the village generally. It also administers the law and village justice. Punishment by a man's equals may not be severe, but it is effective. A bad man is in fact boycotted by his community. Banishment from the village society is regarded in the same light as capital punishment, because such a person cannot be admitted into any other community and becomes a social outcast. The most serious village crimes are those that affect the village welfare—temple vandalism, theft from the gods, running amok, consistent failure to carry out village duties, absence from meetings, incest and even witchcraft.

The Balinese delight in gambling, particularly at cockfights. But gambling is illegal without licence, in Indonesia. However, cockfights are considered on proper occasions to be a part of religious ritual connected with purification by the letting of blood. On these occasions gambling is permitted. Cockfights are held in an open pavilion type of arena under a thatched roof for shade and since they are a part of temple formality, the pavilion, or *wantilan,* is very often located in the outer compound of the village temple. To the average westerner, cockfighting has little interest as a sport or as a spectacle in itself, but no visitor should miss an opportunity to watch the procedure leading up to the actual contests. The lengthy process of challenge between owners, the selection of the final contestants, the attachment of the razor-sharp spurs by binding to the feet, the continual fondling and massaging of the birds by their owners and the final incitement and hackle raising before each fight starts are worth watching. And the excitement when the betting starts has to be seen to be believed.

The village temple or *pura desa* consists essentially of an outer compound entered through an open 'split' gateway (Plate 15), which may include pavilions for food preparation, and a second (and sometimes a third) internal compound entered through a closed-top gateway (Plates 7, 16), in which are located the various shrines to the supreme god and his reincarnations and manifestations, to various spirits, to former leaders and others, and a closed and locked pavilion in which the village records, valuables, masks and costumes and perhaps musical instruments are kept. The *waringin* or sacred banyan tree is also used for religious rites as well as a background for dances and festivals, although many of these are held in the *pura desa* itself.

The market building is simply an open pavilion to provide shade for the stalls and vendors. In many villages the *warin-*

*gin* is substituted, and in some, stalls are simply set up by the vendors in a side street under the shade of woven palm-leaf or woven bamboo shelters. The village market is a focal point of great interest to the visitor, and no opportunity should be lost to stroll in one, to examine the variety and range of goods offered for sale, to savour the smells of coconut oil, dried fish, flowers and spices, and to enjoy moving amongst the crowd of women who are either semi-nude or dressed in most colourful and attractive costumes (Plate 5). Every purchase made calls for bargaining, which lends great animation to the proceedings. In larger towns such as Denpasar itself, the markets are held in permanent locations on concrete floors and are less informal, but nevertheless well worth visiting.

As villages grow in size and importance they divide into smaller sections, similar to the wards of a western city. Each ward really corresponds to one of the original villages making up the larger one and it runs its own affairs just as the village itself does. Each of these subdivisional communities is called a *bandjar*. Each *bandjar* controls its own section of the village property and functions locally with its own council of members under its own leader, the *klian bandjar*. Each *bandjar* takes part in the *desa* activities as a whole. In these cases each *bandjar* will generally have its own small temple, its own meeting place (the *balé bandjar*) and may own some common property for loan to members, the village orchestras, dancing costumes and masks.

Where villages become large enough to become towns, and where these towns become the centres of principalities or regions of government, their character changes markedly. The same basic system of development and government exists but on an expanded scale, with so many repetitive elements as to obscure the central picture, and with the admixture of Chinese and Indian traders and their shops to further colour the scene. In addition the western influence is now becoming noticeable in places such as Denpasar. In these larger towns, where formerly Radjas or Princes held power, they lived in *puri*, or palaces, which still exist although used for other purposes. These palaces were large editions of the village family compound—areas divided into many intercommunicating courtyards surrounded by brick walls, adorned with stone carvings and beautified with trees, gardens and substantial pavilion buildings often ornately carved, including the ancestral shrines. The *puri* of the Radja of Badung can still be seen in Denpasar. This is now an exhibition centre for a number of painters and artists. The *puri* of the Tjokorde of Ubud can be seen at Ubud. This has now become a tourist hotel.

The part played by the *krama desa* as a court of appeal in the village to settle differences and administer the village law has already been discussed. The Balinese prefer to settle their differences at this level and make every effort to do so. Formerly, when these efforts failed, the final appeal was made to the official tribunal at one of the seats of regional government, the *kerta*. The courts of the *kerta* were composed of three Brahmanic priests acting as judges, assisted by lawyers or a prosecutor where necessary. The courts were held in special buildings built on high stone platforms so that the proceedings were visible to all. The Kerta Gosa, the old courthouse of Klungkung, is an example. This famous courthouse is beautifully carved and decorated and the underside of the roof is covered with frescoes depicting the punishments awaiting the wrongdoer in hell. In the *kerta* the law was dispensed strictly according to the rules. The judges reached a decision after hearing all the evidence. No one spoke unless he was addressed by the court. An absentee, or even one whose case was poorly presented, lost his suit. Curiously, the oath was taken by the winner after the verdict was given. This was done at a special religious ceremony conducted for the purpose, and false swearing of an important and serious oath might result in eternal purgatory for the person concerned and all his relations and descendants.

The courts of the *kerta* are mentioned here because every visitor to Bali will wish to visit the famous Kerta Gosa at Klungkung (Plate 49) and will wish to understand its purport. Nowadays, however, the Balinese are subject to the national laws of the Republic of Indonesia administered by courts expressly set up for the purpose by the Government. The new courthouse at Klungkung may be seen adjacent to the old Kerta Gosa. It possesses authority, but no appeal.

# 4

# *The Caste System and Social Order*

The social order was recognised to some extent by the original animist Balinese, the Bali Aga. Living in their walled villages in the mountains they recognised their leaders and their descendants as members of their own primitive aristocracy, with their own rights and authority. The communities of the lowlands recognised rank and position more widely, extending aristocratic status to priests, rulers and some administrators. It was not until Bali came under the Hindu-Javanese rule of the kingdom of Madjapahit after the conquest of Gadja Mada that the Hindu caste system was introduced, albeit on a much less strict basis.

The Hindu castes were never recognised by the Bali Aga villagers, but the villagers of the principalities which then controlled Bali on behalf of the ruler of Madjapahit, introduced a wide range of castes and ranks between the princes and the peasantry. These have now fallen into disuse and today there are four broad ranks of caste recognised in Bali.

Three of these castes belong to the 'nobility'. The high priests are the Brahmanas; the ruling princes and their families and the military class are the Satrias; the merchant class are the Wesias. These castes originate from the gods, for the Indian legends teach that the Brahmanas (the Brahmins of India) came out of the mouth of Brahma, the Satria (Ksatriya) from his arms and the Wesia (Vesiya) from his feet.

The Balinese had always worshipped their ancestors as part of their animistic beliefs. It was not difficult for the new lords of Bali to establish their own kings and princes as gods.

---

PLATE 5. The village market at Sukowati.

PLATE 6. *Kulkul* tower of the temple at Batanbulah (lower left).

PLATE 7. Typical covered gateway, or *padu raksa* to an inner temple area, Se Setan (lower right).

These kings in turn were said to be descended from the deities, or to be reincarnations of them. They were readily accepted by the Balinese as such. It was not unusual formerly, for a prince or a priest to claim divine descent, even from the supreme god, Siwa.

The balance of the Balinese population, comprising some ninety percent of it, belong to the fourth and non-aristocratic caste of the Sudras.

The caste system has become a complex with some Balinese, who will pose as members of a superior caste on occasions in places where they are not known, or who will claim that their former higher caste was lowered as the result of some bad behaviour by an ancestor. In some circumstances, persons of a lower caste have been raised to a higher one.

The highest caste, the Brahmanas, are said to claim descent from the priest Wau Rauh, who created the priesthood of Bali in legend by having many children by his own wives, by their servant women, and in fact by women of all classes. These children became the heads of the Brahmana families. A caste distinction is made between the priests, the initiated Brahmanas, and the uninitiated. Even today there is rivalry between the Brahmanas and the Satrias. The Brahmanas formerly served as judges in the courts (*kertas*), but nowadays have no administrative powers whatsoever. They are forbidden to attend cockfights and are not permitted to make any money in commerce under their own caste rules. The latter consideration, however, is nowadays ignored. Many Brahmanas are prosperous and rich. They can be recognised by the use by the men of the prefix Ida Bagus and by the women of the prefix Ida Ayu before their names, both terms meaning 'high born and beautiful'.

Satrias are theoretically the descendants of the former princes and rulers, many claiming descent from Sri Krisna

---

PLATE 8. Village street at Gutingan showing typical dried-mud walls thatched with rice straw with covered gateways to the individual family compounds.

PLATE 9. Returning the ducks from the rice fields in the early evening. Note the shrines in the rice field dedicated to the goddess of rice and fertility.

C

Kapakisan, ruler of Bali at the time of Gadja Mada's conquest. Satrias are recognised by the use of the prefixes Anak Agung, Tjokorde, Ratu, Prebagus and so on, according to the finer divisions of the caste.

Wesias are known by the prefix title Pregusti or Gusti. They are said to be the descendants of Arya Damar, the predecessor of Gadja Mada, and of other Javanese princes.

The high castes of the artistocracy in Bali confer merely a pleasant social distinction today. Even after centuries of Hindu influence, the princely classes do not rule in the island, and the Hindu philosophy has not been able to displace the rule by independent village communities. But the social distinction conferred by caste is real and often seen. A man cannot marry a woman of a higher caste than himself. For a man to have relations with a woman of a higher caste invited a sentence of death for both in former times, and later of exile. Nowadays special concessions can be made in influential circles by imposing a fine, by annulment, or by lowering the caste of the woman socially. Caste differences affect the social order in the daily relations between persons of different castes. Those of high caste are ever watchful that their inferiors remain at all times at a lower level than themselves. The elevated platforms which form the elevated pavilions in many houses are approached by three or four steps on all sides so that those of lower caste can sit on a lower step than those of superior caste, and it is not unusual to see people move up or down a series of steps when new people join another group.

However, the caste system is not nearly so rigid as that of India, nor so intolerant. The code of etiquette is not unreasonable, and in everyday life the Balinese are friendly, polite and free of undue restrictions. To be accused of bad manners is a serious affront to a Balinese. Personal greetings are simple. Visits are generally accompanied by the bringing of presents, to remove the price tag from which is not good etiquette. Amongst the elderly, the chewing of betel nut is the first act of hospitality, but with the aversion of the young, this practice is dying out. A host must act as servant to his guests, serving meals even though he has servants, eating only after the guests have finished. Visitors from another town or village are expected to stay overnight, perhaps even for several days. These visits may be later repaid, presents being offered in return.

On public occasions, such for instance as weddings, men and women keep themselves in separate groups. When bathing together in the same stream the men will congregate together a little distance from the women. Even in public baths there are separate divisions for men and women. Men will not approach women and lovers are careful not to show their mutual feelings in public, although there is now evidence of a changing attitude in this regard.

Balinese caste etiquette reaches its zenith in regard to the language spoken as between aristocrats and the common people. There are three distinct Balinese languages, the high, the medium and the low. These are not just dialects of the same tongue, but differ entirely in words and derivation. The high tongue is derived from Sanskrit and is of Sanskrit-Javanese origin. It is an expressive language with many fine shades of meaning. It is the language used when addressing a person of high caste. The low tongue is the common every-day Balinese of commerce and is of Malayan origin with some Polynesian influence. It is used by the common people among themselves and by high caste people in addressing commoners. The medium language is used under a wide variety of circumstances. An example would be its use by a person of high caste when addressing an older person of lower caste.

Thus when two Balinese unknown to one another meet, they commence by talking in the high tongue. One of the two will then ask the other his caste. When this has been ascertained, the low caste man will address the high caste man in the high tongue, whilst the high caste man will address the low caste man in the low tongue. Conversation can become very complicated in a company in which men of several different castes are present. A man may not refer to himself in the high tongue whatever the caste of his listener! It is polite to address old people no matter what their caste, in the high tongue, or at least in the medium tongue.

There is still another language, Kawi, used on ritual occasions and in classical writings. It is an ancient form of

Javanese with words predominantly of Sanskrit, and is used today only by the priests.

All Balinese go to school for a few years at least. Initial instruction is in their own language, common Balinese. But after some three years at school the young people must now learn in addition Bahasa Indonesia, a substantially Malay language that has been officially adopted as the *lingua franca* of the Republic. Its use is spreading amongst the younger Balinese because it is much simpler to learn than Balinese and is free of the caste tongues. Strictly speaking a Balinese scholar needs to be able to speak five languages—high, middle, low Balinese; Kawi; and Bahasa Indonesia. And of course the main language of commerce, English, is becoming more and more essential. English is taught from secondary school onward. At high school certain other foreign languages such as French and German may be studied.

PLATE 10. Celebrating the festival of Kuninggan at the Pura Taman Sari at Mas.

PLATE 11. Shrine dedicated to the village ancestors, or *gedong pesimpangan*, Temple of Taman Ajun at Mengwi.

# 5

# *Religion and Rites*

The animistic religion of the ancient Balinese arose as do most primitive religious concepts, from the need to interpret phenomena not at that time understood, and therefore regarded as supernatural. The sun, the moon, the sea, fire, water and wind, the earth, the mountains, the trees and crops and so on were endowed with magic and said to be inhabited by spirits. The spirit world was extended to inanimate concepts such as fertility and sickness and led inevitably to the deification of ancestors.

We have already seen how this simple concept was influenced by the transfer from Java of Buddhist and Hindu practices modified by early Javanese animism, so that the religion of Bali is now described as a Hindu-Bali one. Whilst Hindu gods and Hindu rites are in evidence, however, it seems clear that the primitive animist practices of the early Balinese have remained dominant. While Siwa, Wisnu and Brahma are accepted as the greatest of the gods, they are never present in concrete form. There are no images of the gods seen in any of the temples. When they are present in the temple they are there only in spirit, and are therefore never seen. Facilities are provided only for the spirits of the gods to rest in appropriate shrines. There are no idols and no idolatry. It is the spirits of the Hindu gods that are deified, not the gods themselves, and their spirits take their place in the temples along with the spirits of ancestors, of the mountains, of abundance, of fertility and many others.

---

PLATE 12. Shrines in a family compound at Mas showing the elaborate decoration and high quality of construction common to the sanctuaries of wealthy families.

PLATE 13. Women dressed in typical costumes, *kains* and *kebajas*, bringing offerings of food to the temple at Gelgel.

The Balinese live with their forefathers in a family union of the living and the spirits of the dead.

The Brahmanic high priests, or *pedandas*, whose utterances and bell-ringing ritual are derived from Hindu practice, remain apart from the common Balinese community, who have their own simple priests, the temple servants, or *pemangkus*, whose function is mainly to guard the temples, sweep them and keep them clean, and to preside on festive occasions.

To the Balinese, religion is closely bound up with nationality. If he changes faith, he ceases to be a 'Balinese'. Conversely no person of another nationality, whose forefathers must inevitably belong to that nationality for all time, can be converted to the Balinese religion and become of 'Balinese' nationality. To the Balinese also, their religion represents the law, since it dictates the rules of behaviour and is the basis of village life. The welfare and prosperity of the community must be ensured by religious rites designed to please and foster the spirits of righteousness, and to ensure continuing guidance and protection by ancestors. The forces of evil which cause sickness and want, and promote bestiality and vandalism, must be placated by suitable offerings, and ritual steps must be taken to keep the village free of demons and witches and other evil spirits of a troublesome nature.

These rites consist in the main of festivals held at the village temple, especially on selected holidays and on the anniversary of the temple itself. On these occasions, magnificently displayed offerings of food are taken to the temple by the women, and entertainment in the form of music, dancing and drama is provided in order to attract and encourage the ancestors of the village to remain among the people. Every day such a festival is held somewhere among the villages and it is a colourful sight in the late afternoon to see the gaily dressed women proceeding to the temple in procession, carrying the offerings on their heads (Plates 4, 40) and followed by the musicians and the villagers.

Provision of these festivals, initiated as religious rites, became of necessity community affairs. They required organisation and the participation of all members of the village community. This inevitably led to a cooperative system of community life and the development of the village council ruling on behalf of the ancestral spirits to whom, originally, all land and the wealth it represented, belonged. An outline of this village life and administration has already been given. It is sufficient here only to stress its interdependence with Balinese religion.

The visitor to Bali will notice at once that in spite of the fact that there are more temples in relation to the population than anywhere else on earth, there are no temples in the normal sense. There are no buildings to be entered where images and idols of the gods are displayed and worshipped. In Bali, every household has a temple area, a small walled-off portion of the family compound in which are located a number of small shrines (Plate 12) dedicated to the mountains, the family forebears and to propitious spirits. In the ordinary village compounds these shrines are simple, of wood or bamboo, with roofs thatched with sago-palm fibre. In the compounds of the well-to-do the shrines may be of brick and carved stone and may become very ornate and elaborate, but nevertheless have the same simple basic principle of a resting place for the spirit in an enclosure, or in the case of the supreme deity, Siwa, the god of Gunung Agung, a symbolic chair for the accommodation of the spirit when it is present in the temple. In the houses of princes and in the temples of the larger villages and towns the arrangement is exactly the same, but the degree of elaboration increases, the temple compounds being walled in brick with stone carving, sometimes simple in character, sometimes extremely elaborate. There are temples in the cemeteries, temples in the rice fields, on beaches, in caves, on cliffs, on mountains and in forests. Temples are everywhere, but in all cases they are structures of great beauty and interest and their detail is well worth studying as a distinctive art form.

Every temple differs from every other temple in some of its details. No two are alike, but there is in general a typical scheme of arrangement which is always broadly followed. The main elements of a Balinese temple are shown diagrammatically in Fig. 2. There are usually two courtyards, an outer one entered by the typical Balinese 'split' gateway (Plate 15), known as a *tjandi bentar* (A), and an inner one entered by

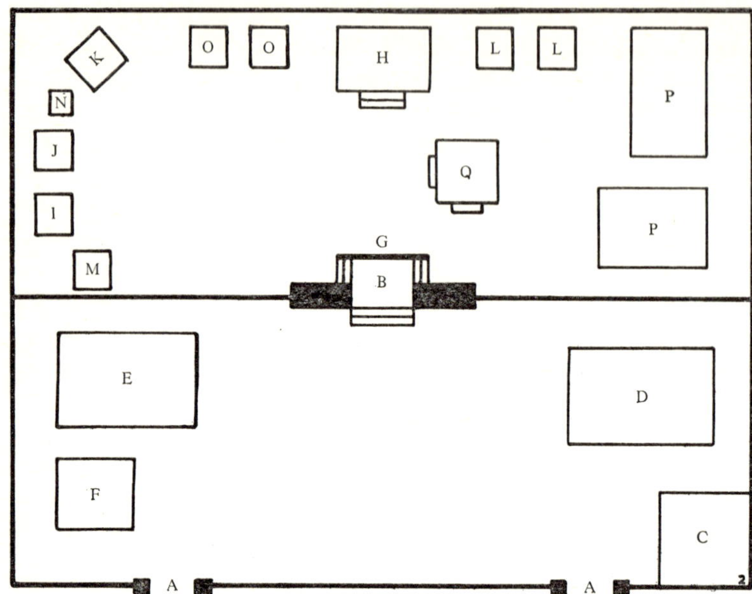

2. Typical arrangement of a Balinese temple. A, *Tjandi bentar*, a 'split' gate. B, *Padú raksa*, a covered gateway. C, *Kulkul*, tower. D, Cooking pavilion. E, Pavilion for the preparation of offerings. F, Pavilion for the orchestra. G, *Aling aling* wall. H, *Gedong pesimpangan*, or shrine to the founder of the village. I, J, Shrines to the mountains. K, *Padmasana*. L, Shrines to representatives of the gods. M, Niche for Taksu. N, Shrine to Madjapahit. O, Temple shrines. P, *Balé piasan*, or pavilion for offerings. Q, *Paruman*, a resting place for all the gods.

a covered gateway (Plates 7, 16, 45) of a more ornate type, the *padú raksa* (B). In some of the larger temples there are three successive compounds, one outer and two inner. In either case the innermost compound is the holy place of the temple containing the actual shrines.

The outer compound usually contains the *kulkul* tower, the village 'bell' tower (C), and several simple pavilions, one for cooking food (D), one for use in preparing offerings (E), and one for the use of the *gamelan* orchestra (F). The outer courtyard is used for music, dancing and entertainment on festive occasions and generally bears little ornament.

The *padú raksa* (B) leading to the inner courtyard has a pair of wooden doors, often elaborately carved, and is approached up steps leading to an elevated sill facing which is a wall (G). Access to the inner court is by steps leading down from the elevated sill on either side. The wall (G) across the gate, the *aling aling*, is put there to prevent the entry of evil spirits, who only travel in straight lines and who on entering the gateway come up against the *aling aling*, become confused, turn round and go out again. The *padú raksa* is the most notable feature in nearly all temples, being massive in design and ornately decorated with fantastically detailed stone carvings interlain with the soft pink characteristic brick of the island. In general outline it is similar in shape to the outer gate, the *tjandi bentar*, and both bear a similarity to the normal Balinese representation of the universe, a wide base surmounted by a succession of receding platforms representing the mountains leading up to the heavens. The outer gate, being of typical 'split' style, thus may be said to represent the splitting of the universe. The visitor to Bali will quickly become familiar with these typical gateway designs, seen in every temple in every town and village.

The inner courtyard of the temple contains the shrines. These are usually arranged in rows along the 'north' wall (towards the mountain) and the 'east' wall, these directions being considered the most holy. The shrines are small platforms containing resting places for the spirits of the gods when visiting the temple and are usually roofed with thatch of sago-palm fibre, *idjuk*. Some shrines are built with multiple thatched roofs in the style of a pagoda. The roofs are always of an odd number, from three to eleven, and are constructed round a central open wooden shaft down which the spirit can enter. These shrines are known as *merus* (Plates 19, 52) and are quite spectacular when seen in quantity. The Mother Temple at Besakih on the slopes of Mt. Agung consists almost entirely of *merus* and in the Water Temple at Mengwi there are a number of magnificent examples with elaborately carved bases. In the normal village temple there will usually be only one, with three roofs. Such a *meru* is dedicated to Dewi Sri, the goddess of rice. Five roofs show dedication to Iswara, a reincarnation of Siwa. Seven roofs show dedication to Brahma, nine roofs to Wisnu and eleven roofs to the supreme god, Siwa.

In the middle of the 'eastern' side is usually a masonry building with an elaborate staircase leading to a platform in front of its doors which are finely carved and kept locked. This is the *gedong pesimpangan* (H), dedicated to the village founder and which is used to house the relics, heirlooms, statues, bronzes and other valuable possessions of the village, perhaps including the village masks and costumes (Plates 11, 14).

Two shrines (I, J) are dedicated to the spirit of the mountains, Gunung Agung and Gunung Batur (or Gunung Batukau). They have one roof only, ending in phallic points on occasion. The *padmasana* (K) is the most important shrine, which stands in the 'northeast' corner oriented with its back towards the Gunung Agung. This is a shrine shaped in the form of the universe, with a base often carved to represent the turtle and entwined snakes motif which supports the universe, surmounted by receding platforms representing the mountains and topped by a stone chair with a high back (Plate 17). This is for the supreme god, Siwa. In many large temples the *padmasana* is equipped with three chairs side by side for Siwa, Wisnu and Brahma, the trinity of gods.

Two shrines (L) are usually included for the representatives of the deities who ensure that the proper offerings are made, and there is a stone niche (M) for Taksu, who conveys the gods' decisions to the people when necessary through mediums. Finally there is a shrine dedicated to the gods of those who came from Madjapahit (N), which generally carries the sculpture of a deer's head or antlers. In addition there may be shrines appropriate to a particular temple (O).

While these shrines represent those which are normally present, many of them are quite often absent and others not listed are present. The variety of deities and spirits is so extensive and personal preferences in worship are so divergent, that great variation in the dedication of temple and family shrines exists, and no hard and fast rules can be laid down.

Other pavilions may be present in the inner courtyard. These are simple sheds for temple offerings, known as *balé piasan* (P), and a central pavilion (Q), known as the *paruman* which serves as a communal resting place for all the gods.

It is usual for every Balinese village community to have some simple shrine or temple area, the *pura puseh*, or navel temple, the original simple village temple; the *pura desa*, or town temple, serving to provide a place for official celebrations and festivals for the whole village; and the *pura dalem*, the Temple of the Dead, built in the village cemetery. In the case of villages which have become subdivided, each *bandjar* has its own temple. There are also temples in the rice fields (*pura bedugul*), which serve the agricultural cooperatives, the *subaks* (Plates 45, 46).

Balinese temples are normally deserted except for the presence of the temple keeper, or *pemangku*, dressed in white clothes, who sweeps and cleans it and officiates at temple feasts. The Brahmanic priests, the *pedandas*, do not take any active part in the temple on festive occasions as a rule, but may do so on special occasions. It is only on those occasions when a festival or feast is being prepared that the temple becomes filled with activity (Plate 10), and it is only when such a festival takes place that the community flocks to the temple and uses it. The temples of Bali are quiet, pleasant places, full of charm and interest, packed with architectural features and carved adornment. As long as the temple area is treated with due respect, the visitor is free to enter at any time, and to enjoy the restful atmosphere.

The principal festival in any village is the occasion on which the temple celebrates its 'birthday', which is held on the anniversary of its original consecration. The Balinese 'year' consists of twelve months, each of thirty-five days, a total of 420 days. A Balinese has two 'birthdays' in each year, that is, one every 210 days. Temple 'anniversaries' follow the same rule. Everybody takes part. For days before, the men prepare the temple precincts, building temporary bamboo altars and tables (a sight frequently seen in the villages), erecting decorations and cooking food, which is always prepared by the men on these occasions. Meanwhile the women prepare the temple offerings, which are blessed by the *pemangku* as they are brought to the temple in procession by the women, who carry them on their heads. The people pray, flinging flowers in the direction of the shrines and the *pemangku* anoints them with holy water. Meantime, outside the temple, the people listen to the music of the orchestras, watch dramatic performances and even stage cockfights, which become a part of the ritual. The gods are persuaded by the priest to enter the bodies of the temple *artjas*. These are male and female figures made either from carved and painted wood or from old coins (*kepengs*) sewn together, and are usually kept in the *gedong pesimpangan*. These are symbolic of the gods, and are taken in procession, led by women carrying offerings and pots of holy water, shaded by umbrellas and followed by the men and orchestras, to the sea or to a river if the sea is too far away. Here they are given a symbolic bath or cleansing (*melis*). After this the procession returns to the village. Here the *artjas* are received back by the *pemangku* with ritual requiring purification of the ground by holy water and the gift of further offerings of food, the essence of which is wafted in the direction of the *artjas* by the priest.

Throughout the night the festivities continue with plays, music and dancing. During the night the *djéro Taksú* is asked to inform the people through mediums who transmit its advice whilst entranced with its spirit, whether the offerings made have been well received by the gods. At dawn the festival concludes with a ceremony in honour of the rising sun, after which the essence of the food having been consumed by the gods, the offerings are collected by the women and taken home for family consumption.

The great festival of Njepi marks the celebration of the Balinese solar new year. It is held at the spring equinox and

---

PLATE 14. *Gedong pesimpangan*, or shrine to the village ancestors at Batubulan. The black and white check material draped on the two guardian figures, *saput poleng*, is considered to have magical powers to frighten evildoers away.

PLATE 15. Split gate, or *tjandi bentar*, which is the normal entrance gate to the forecourt of a temple. This example at Gelgel is unusual in that the opposing faces are carved and decorated (lower left).

PLATE 16. Example of a highly ornamented covered gateway, or *padu raksa*, leading to the inner sanctuary of the Pura Taman Sari at Mas (lower right).

marks the beginning of spring and the end of the rainy season. But more importantly it is a ceremony of a special nature designed to clean out the island and to drive out all devils which have fallen on Bali following the sweeping of all devils out of hell by Yama, the god of Hades. Njepi itself is a day of complete rest which follows the actual ceremony of purification. No fires, no work, no cooking and no sexual intercourse are permitted on that day. For this reason the days immediately prior to Njepi are occupied with busy preparations for the festival. Altars and stagings are erected, food is prepared to last through the festival, and *melis* processions to take the spirits of the gods to the sea for purification and cleansing are held. The great purification, the *metjaru*, takes place on the day before Njepi. On this day cockfighting is permitted, for the blood spilt acts as a sacrifice to divert the evil spirits and preserve the land. This provides an opportunity for a little gambling and the dead roosters are taken home and cooked for Njepi. Before sundown the evil spirits are attracted to the *metjaru* which includes a great offering before the altars of food of all sorts, strong liquor, money, household goods, samples of every seed and fruit growing on the island, and samples of the flesh of every wild and domestic animal. These offerings are all arranged in the shape of an eight-pointed star aligned with the Balinese cardinal points. Brahmanic priests are employed to carry out the mystic rites by chanting magic formulae, gesturing and bell ringing. After luring all the evil spirits to the offering by this means they are then thrown out by the curses put on them by the priests and by continued noise from *kulkuls*, drums, gongs and tin cans, and by the shouting and yelling of the people. The noise continues far into the night until it is felt that all devils have been driven out. Njepi the following day is strictly observed in

---

PLATE 17. *Padmasana,* or shrine dedicated to the supreme god Siwa, at the Temple of Taman Ajun at Mengwi. The shrine is surmounted by a carved stone seat for the spirit of the god to rest on. The back of this seat faces towards Mt. Agung.

PLATE 18. The moat of the inner sanctuary of the Water Temple, Taman Ajun, at Mengwi showing the base portions of *merus* dedicated to Siwa.

most villages where traffic comes to a standstill and villagers remain in their houses. Even in Denpasar itself, although people may visit and there may be some games organised for the amusement of young people, observance of Njepi is very strict.

The Balinese celebrate another very important holy day called Galunggan when the ancestral spirits make an 'annual' pilgrimage to earth to reinhabit the homes of their descendants. This is followed ten days later by the feast of all souls, Kuninggan. These festivals are celebrated with offerings of food, processions and music in a manner similar to the temple festivals and at the same interval of 210 days. At Galunggan the streets and houses are decorated with *lamaks* (Plate 35) and *pendjors*, made from various coloured palm leaves and bamboo. The *barongs* (Plate 37) are allowed to roam and dance in the streets of the villages accompanied by orchestral music. The *barongs* are mythical animals in the form of a Chinese lion with long hair and snapping jaws, animated by two men, one at the head and one at the tail, which are the central attraction of the Barong Dance, described in a later chapter. Kuninggan corresponds with the temple feast of Tirta Empul, the sacred baths near Tampaksiring, where people bathe in the purifying waters of the holy spring which emanates from spouts set in figures carved in the walls of the public baths. On the following day a big celebration takes place at Sakenan temple on Turtle Island just off the coast at Sanur.

The Balinese religion recognises spirits of all kinds. There are spirits of good and evil, gods and demons, banded into two opposing groups so that there is continuous conflict between them. All spirits are imbued with magic powers, and the eternal struggle between good and evil inevitably affects the daily life of the Balinese. They must propitiate both sides in this struggle so as to avoid neglect by the good spirits and retribution by the bad spirits. It is important that a balanced control of spirit influence be maintained in the interests of harmonious village life. The influence of the gods that produce good fortune, good health and fertility is counterbalanced by the influence of the evil spirits that bring misfortune, bad health and famine. There are times when individuals, or families, or even the village become more prone to the influence of evil, such as at childbirth, menstruation, death, or when a crime has been committed or temple vandalism has occurred. If for these reasons a person or a community becomes physically weakened or religiously unclean (*sebel*), cleansing and purifying ceremonies must be held to restore the balance of good over evil. This is done by making offerings, purification by fire and water, and by the incantation of secret and magic formulae by consecrated priests, or *pedandas*. Very many Balinese rituals are of this nature.

There are many demons and devils in the Balinese spirit world. Some are the inoffensive giants of legend, the *raksasas*, but the *butas* and *kalas* are the evil spirits of malice and dissension that haunt the sea shore, the depths of the forest, isolated places and the crossroads of the village. Their purpose is to disturb and pollute, to persecute and destroy, to promote sickness and ill-health.

Gifts to the gods must be sumptuous and well-presented. They must be offered on suitable altars and consist as do presents given to human beings, of gifts of foods, flowers, meats and money. Offerings intended for evil spirits, however, are contemptuously thrown on the ground and are generally of offal. The gods consume the essence of the offerings, wafted towards them by the priests. The villagers take home and eat the material remainder. Offerings to appease evil spirits, however, being polluted in themselves, are left for the dogs to consume. There are special occasions set aside on every fifth and fifteenth day for appeasing the evil spirits, but little offerings—a few grains of rice, a few *kepengs*, a few flowers—will, by virtue of their greed, keep them occupied and minimise their evil actions.

It is clear that if conditions in the village are such that the evil spirits become dominant, serious troubles will ensue. This situation can result in epidemics of sickness, the loss of crops and other misfortunes, death and destruction. Under these conditions most elaborate and costly ceremonies of purification with offerings of blood are necessary to effect that purification. Whilst the Balinese are content to use their temple attendants for most purposes, these difficult and complicated rites of purification must be carried out by Brahmanic priests, or *pedandas*, who have been trained since youth and instructed in the magic ritual and language of the priests by a *pedanda* as master and finally ordained to the priesthood. They are exclusively of Brahmanic caste. They used to act as judges in the courts and being substantially the only people able to understand the several complicated Balinese calendars, are consulted when it is necessary to determine an auspicious day for commencing a specific project, such as building a temple or a house, holding a wedding ceremony or a cremation. They are essential to the ceremonies of the nobility for caste reasons, but even the poorest commoner will employ a *pedanda* if he is able to, particularly at cremation, when it is important to ensure that his dead are correctly inducted into the heavens.

Balinese Brahmanas all claim descent from the mythical Wau Rauh, high priest of Madjapahit, who came to Bali and by taking many wives from various castes established the Brahmanic clans. *Pedandas* dedicate their lives to their theological studies and to the practice of their magic rituals, which they maintain with great secrecy. These rituals have been handed down through the Sanskrit writings of the Hindus containing the powerful magic formulae recited with mysterious sounds, accompanied by bell ringing, flower throwing and the sprinkling of holy water. Holy water itself is made by the *pedandas* from ordinary water by the use of these magic formulae. Its properties and its effect are much more powerful than those of holy water obtained from holy springs in the mountains or from the crater lake.

In spite of the introduction of Brahministic ritual, in spite of the influence of the Hindu cult and of early contact with

PLATE 19. *Merus* at the Water Temple, Taman Ajun, at Mengwi thatched with *idjuk*, the fibre of the sago palm (upper left).

PLATE 20. Carved statue of the witch Rangda at the *pura desa* of Parmidjoan showing the typical charactertistics—canine teeth, bulging eyes, long fingernails, enormous tongue and large sagging breasts (upper right).

PLATE 21. The Pura Langon at Ubud and its attractive reflecting pool. Here the souls of the members of the Royal Family of Ubud may rest after cremation.

the religious beliefs of the Chinese, Indians and Javanese, the Balinese religion remains substantially as animistic now as it has ever been in the past. The Balinese worship the sun, the earth and water as the sources of life. Fire is a purifying element. The mountains are a source of fertility where the gods themselves dwell, for which reason the mountains are revered in every temple and family shrine. The highest mountain, the Gunung Agung, is the pinnacle of the universe, the central focal point of worship, the house of Siwa the supreme deity. It reaches to the heavens from where the spirits of their ancestors return to earth and periodically to their homes as honoured guests. No idols are worshipped, and images of the gods are considered holy only when temporarily inhabited by the spirits of the gods, which are, of course, invisible.

Evil spirits are inevitably always present and must be pacified with appropriate offerings to avoid illness and misfortune. The religious life of the Balinese is very closely integrated with their community life, and provides an example of the eternal struggle between good and evil. Good positive forces are encouraged by propitiation of the gods through proper rituals and proper offerings, observance of the laws of community life, community service and avoidance of crime. Evil or negative forces are derived from the actions of evil spirits dwelling in unclean places, ready to cause illness, misfortune and destruction should the community become weak and vulnerable by becoming unclean, and are removed by ritual purification of the land, or of individuals, or of the village. Thus the eternal struggle between good and evil which is basic to the Balinese religious concept, provides the essentials on which Balinese community life and respect for the law have been built up. The two are inseparably linked.

---

PLATE 22. Woman weaving silken scarf at Mas. This is a typical Balinese loom with the warp tensioned by means of a spring bow across the back of the weaver.

PLATE 23. *Umah metén*, sleeping quarters for the head of the family or for the women alone, in the family compound of a well-to-do Balinese. Note the small bamboo shrine in front marking the burial place of the afterbirth of a child of the family.

D

# 6

# *Domestic Life*

The Balinese family dwelling consists of a small complex of simple buildings erected within the family compound. The compound is surrounded by a wall of sun-baked mud protected from rain damage by a roofing of thatch, sometimes of palm leaf but more commonly of rice straw. There is normally only one entrance through a raised gateway defined by side pillars of mud surmounted by a lintel and thatched roof. In front of the gate, on each side of it, are two small shrines or niches used for offerings. Just inside the gate is a wall, the *aling aling* which is designed, as in the case of the village temple, to prevent the entrance of evil spirits.

Within the compound a number of small buildings of simple construction are placed according to the same rules which govern the construction of the village temple, and indeed the village itself. The family may live on its own, or there may be several related families living together within one enclosure. All will pray at the same common family temple located in an internal courtyard within the family compound. The family temple must be placed on the 'northeast' corner of the compound, and the shrines within it must be placed in accordance with established practice. The individual buildings within the compound are designed to meet the needs of the families in residence, and may be readily added to, since they are constructionally simple. They are normally made of bamboo, palm leaf and grass thatch. The compound generally contains some coconut trees, bananas, papayas and other fruits and has a few flowers and perhaps a frangipanni tree to provide decoration. The ground is of bare hardened earth kept well-swept and clean.

A typical family compound is shown in Fig. 3. It is entered by the gateway (A) with *aling aling* wall (B) to block the entry of evil spirits. In the 'northeast' corner is the court-

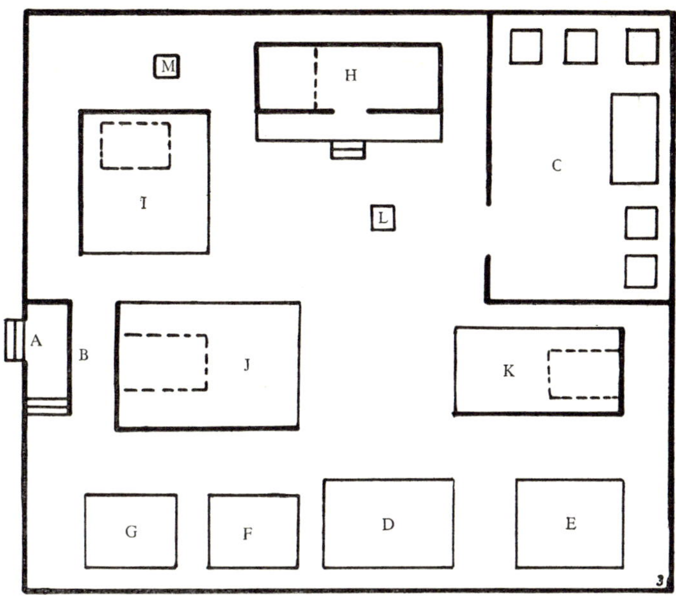

3. Typical family compound. A, Entrance gate. B, *Aling aling* wall. C, Family temple area. D, *Paon*, or kitchen. E, *Lumbung*, or rice granary. F, Chicken coop. G, Pigsty. H, *Umah metén*, sleeping quarters for the head of the family. I, *Balé tiang sanga*, or social pavilion. J, K, Sleeping pavilions. L, M, *Tugu* shrines.

yard forming the family temple area (C) where simple shrines of bamboo and grass thatch are located. The main shrine is dedicated to the ancestral spirits. Other shrines are dedicated to the mountains, to *taksu* the interpreter of the gods, and to *ngurah* the administrator for the gods. There may also be additional shrines of special significance appropriate to the particular families concerned and their individual needs. The kitchen, the *paon* (D) is located on the 'south' side of the compound (towards the sea) and must be at a lower level than the bedrooms and living quarters. The kitchen is a simple building of four posts with a thatched roof and earthen floor. It contains a bamboo table for the preparation of food, and a crude 'stove' built up of mud on which the food is cooked over smouldering fires of charcoal and forest debris. The kitchen is substantially enclosed by walls in most cases and is usually dark and hot. In lowland villages it is separated from the other buildings of the compound as described here, but in mountain villages where the nights are cold, the cooking is done in the same building which houses the sleeping quarters, and provides a welcome warmth.

Located on the 'south' side of the compound alongside the kitchen, is the *lumbung*, or rice granary (E), where the family's supply of unhusked rice is kept bound up in sheaves just as it was brought in from the rice fields. The construction of the *lumbung* varies considerably, but it normally consists of a walled platform with a steep thatched roof. The platform is supported by four wooden posts each provided with a wide circular disc of wood as a capping, to prevent the ingress of rats. A chicken coop (F) and a covered area in which the pig may be tethered (G) complete the 'southern' side of the compound.

On the 'northern' side of the compound the *umah metén* (H) has pride of place. This is the most important building in the compound after the shrine area, and is the sleeping quarters for the head of the family and his wife (Plate 23). This is generally the only fully-enclosed building in the compound. It is windowless and has doors that can be locked to ensure complete privacy. The doors often open onto a small verandah-like platform which is approached by steps. The *metén* must of course be at a higher level than any of the other buildings in the compound to preserve its relative status. The building is not only the sleeping quarters of the heads of the family into which they lock themselves at night, but it also serves as the repository for the family heirlooms, jewellery and gold, and very often money may be kept buried in the earthen floor under the bed.

The remaining buildings in the compound are all open type pavilions with wall panels on one or two sides as a rule. The *balé tiang sanga* (I) is the equivalent of the family parlour and is also the guest house. It is generally equipped with bamboo-covered benches, which serve as seats where the guests can sit cross-legged while eating, and which can be used as beds for guests with temporary screening in place. Two other *balés*, or pavilions (J and K) are shown in Fig. 3. These are the pavilions used by relatives and children for sleeping, and will vary in size and number according to family requirements.

The typical *balé* is a simple and elegant structure. The floor is raised above ground level in the form of a platform which is usually approached on all open sides by a series of three or four continuous steps. We have already seen that these steps serve a useful function in providing different levels for people of different caste to sit. The platform may be of bare earth in a simple family compound, but in the compound of the well-to-do it will be paved with brick, stone or tiling—all long-wearing and cool materials. The roof is a thick thatch of *alang alang* grass tied to the ribs of coconut leaves with sago-palm fibre. These are in turn lashed to the bamboo rafters using the same material. The thatch is perhaps twelve to eighteen inches thick. It is long-lasting, even in the face of many rainy seasons, and provides coolness in the pavilion underneath it. It is supported on a timber structure set on posts rising from the platform. The structure is carefully built using halved and slotted joints pegged together with the heartwood of the coconut palm. The posts, which may vary in number from four to twelve according to the status and importance of the *balé*, are cut to a standard length of seven feet, and it is an inviolable rule that the wood of the post must be oriented from base to cap in the same direction as that in which it grew in the tree it was cut from. The posts and roof timbers in the homes of the wealthy are often elaborately carved. In wealthy homes also, the walls, where used, may be constructed of brick with panels of intricate stone carving.

Finally in the centre of the compound will be a small shrine (L) dedicated to the spirit of the land, where offerings will be made before the day's work begins, and another (M) 'west' of the *metén*. These shrines are known as *tugú*.

The house compound of wealthy Balinese is laid out according to the same basic principles. The family shrine is located on the 'northeast' corner, the *metén* on the 'north' side, the kitchen, granary and animals on the 'south' side. The relative elevations of the pavilions and buildings are carefully preserved in order of importance. The difference lies mainly in the type of construction, its quality and adornment, and in the general beautification of the compound. The walls surrounding the compound will be of brick ornamented with carved stone. The gate will be an elegant 'split' type as used on the temples. The kitchen, granary and animals will be further removed from the family pavilion by virtue mainly of the larger size of the compound. The pavilions will be constructed of brick and stone and will have carved posts and roofs. The guest pavilion will be separate from the family one and will often be constructed in the form of a *metén*, being partly open, and partly enclosed by four walls with a door opening onto the open section. There may even be a special pavilion reserved for important family occasions, such as weddings, childbirth and funerals. The compound is often well-developed with paving, carved figures and other embellishment, and will incorporate more trees and flowers of a decorative nature.

The palaces, *puri*, of the former princes, are laid out also observing the same basic rules that govern the design of the village compound. They differ only in that they are much larger in size again, and in that they are usually composed of a series of interconnecting courtyards. The outer courtyard is generally unoccupied and entered through a 'split' gate. From this the inner section of the palace is entered through a raised covered gate fitted with wooden doors, a *padú raksa*, as is the inner courtyard of a temple. Such palace gates are equally as large and ornate as in most temples. Similar but smaller gates will lead from courtyard to courtyard throughout the compound. The various walled-off sections were formerly designed as living compartments with pavilion sleeping quarters and often kitchens, for the Radja's numerous wives and for his various relatives and dependants. Some of these courts are well decorated with gardens, shrubs, lily ponds and so on, while others are given over to food preparation and cooking, weaving, orchestral practice and other activities. The family shrines will be housed in the 'northeast' corner in a courtyard which may be one of two or three forming the temple area. The shrines will usually be of elegant design in brick and stone construction. Good examples of the palaces of former princes may be seen in Denpasar (the *puri* Pemetjutan) and in Ubud (the *puri* of the Tjokorde Agung). The latter is now a tourist hotel where guests may stay in an old-style Balinese atmosphere.

Whatever the size or quality of a compound its construction may not be commenced except on a propitious day which must be determined by reference to the Balinese calendar as interpreted by a priest. In fact no pavilion, building or shrine within the compound may be built at other than a propitious time. To ignore this principle would be, in the Balinese view, to invite disaster.

It should be noted that while the majority of existing family compounds are laid out in accordance with the established principles outlined above, there is now a tendency to arrange new compounds with more variety and in ways designed to comply more with family desires than with traditional convention.

Family life begins at the first sign of dawn. The women sweep the yard and fetch water for the day from the wells or from the village spring. The men put out the bamboo cages of the fighting cocks in the street so that the roosters can enjoy the movement and forage in the fresh green grass on which the cages are placed. After bathing, the men start for the fields to attend to the rice crops, taking with them small packets of boiled rice in banana-leaf containers. This food will support them until they return at midday, although it is not unusual nowadays to see itinerant food vendors on the roadside where rice harvesting is going on, providing extra nourishment for the workers. The women set out unhusked sheaves of rice from the granary to dry in the sun, and start the fire for the day's cooking.

The staple village food is basically boiled rice (*nasi*) eaten cold with a little bit of fish or meat, salt, grated coconut and chilli peppers. This frugal meal seems to suffice in the main, but it is supplemented as required, and particularly on festive occasions, with vegetables, meats and other delicacies prepared with a large variety of hot spices. As soon as the rice is cooked in the morning, the women prepare little squares of banana leaf each containing a few grains of rice, salt and a flower. These are offerings intended to placate the evil spirits, and are placed in front of each house unit, in front of the family shrine, in front of the altar in the centre of the compound, and at the gate. These offerings are soon eaten by the hungry dogs or ants, but this does not affect their power.

Around midday the men return from work in the fields and partake of a hot lunch of rice and chilli sauce, eating in silence by hand from a banana leaf. Water is normally drunk after the meal. The women eat after the men have finished.

In the afternoon the men will sleep or chat in the *balé bandjar* before returning to work in the late afternoon. During this rest period many of the men will be seen gently massaging and fondling their fighting cocks. The women spend the afternoon weaving, threshing rice, or delousing one another's hair, a pastime that can be seen going on at almost any time.

Hand weaving is an art widely practised by the women of the village, and it may be seen being carried on in the pavilions attached to the larger houses and palaces, in many of the wayside galleries where paintings and carvings are exhibited (Plate 22), and in many temple precincts. The cotton used is spun and dyed locally. The loom is of the very simplest type. A wooden frame supports a beam on which the warp is tied, the other (woven) end being attached to a bamboo roller in front of the weaver. This stick is tied at each end to the ends of a springy bow-shaped yoke supported from the weaver's back, so that by leaning backwards the warp is tensioned and by leaning forwards it is slackened. The weft is carried in a bamboo shuttle which is passed from side to side by hand, the warp threads being alternately raised and lowered by hand-tied healds and held in position for every weft motion by a bamboo stick. A hand operated comb is used to consolidate the weave.

Plain striped patterns are produced by selected colours in the warp or weft or both, but there is one traditional style of weaving still seen in Bali which is of special interest. This style of weaving employs a method known as *ikat*. The weft, dyed to the colour of the pattern, is assembled on a frame of the size of the piece of cloth to be woven. The desired pattern is then delineated by wrapping water-impervious fibre around the threads. The weft is then redyed to the base colour of the cloth, the protected threads remaining the original colour desired for the pattern. When carefully woven together with the warp, the desired pattern is reproduced on the finished cloth. Because of the error of positioning inherent in the method, the pattern shows a characteristic lack of definition which gives the finished cloth an unusual appearance and a special appeal. When the weft alone is pattern-dyed in this way the cloth is known as *endek*. It may be seen being woven at the *puri* Pemetjutan in Denpasar and in other places. When both warp and weft are pattern-dyed the effect is even more pleasing and attractive, and when produced in this way the cloth is known as *grinsing*. *Grinsing* is exclusively a product of the village of Tenganan.

Threshing is done towards evening when the sun-dried rice is prepared for use the following day. Two or more women generally husk the rice by pounding it with long, heavy wooden pestles dropped rhythmically into wooden mortars. The husks are separated from the grain by centrifugal winnowing in a shallow tray.

When the day's work is done, the women and men both bathe again, put on clean clothes, put blossoms in the hair and relax until sundown when the second meal of the day is taken. After this the evening may be spent talking or listening to the orchestra rehearsing, or at a feast or theatrical performance if either is being held.

The basic boiled rice with chilli pepper sauce is supplemented by many attractive and tasty embellishments of a type common to eastern countries. Roast chicken, duck and pork are the meats most commonly eaten, but additional delicacies are ant-eaters, flying fox, lizards, squid, rice birds (eaten whole), crayfish, fish and turtle. All are cooked and served with a variety of sauces made up of spices of all sorts chopped and prepared with aromatic roots and leaves, onions, garlic, fish paste, grated coconut, lime juice and peppers. These sauces are always strong in flavour and are usually very hot. Corn and sweet potatoes, marrow, beans and other vegetables are available and there is a wide variety of fruits, including papaya, bananas, pineapples, mangoes, oranges, melons, jackfruit, durien, mangosteen and rambutan.

While the women prepare the everyday food of the household, it is the men alone who prepare the dishes for the festivals when sea turtle and sucking pig are the main attractions. The former is prepared in several ways by chopping up the meat and cooking it with grated coconut and spices flavoured with tamarind leaves or coconut cream or raw turtle's blood diluted with lime juice. This delicacy is called *lawar*. The latter is prepared by stuffing with spices and spit roasting very slowly over a light fire. Another essential delicacy at banquets and festivals is *saté lilit*, a paste of meat, spices and coconut cream, which is roasted over charcoal on bamboo sticks. Of course, ordinary *saté* made by roasting little pieces of chicken or pork on bamboo skewers, which are eaten after dipping in a peanut based sauce, is eaten as well.

Turtles are generally seen displayed for sale on the side of the road approaching Pesangganan where the long causeway reaches out towards Benoa, the port of Denpasar. They are bought alive and kept alive until it is time to prepare them for eating. A small turtle costs in the vicinity of $US 5 and large ones up to $US 15.

At banquets, the rice, garnished with vegetables and meats, and with spices, peanuts, grated coconut and other condiments, is served to the guests on square trays made of banana leaf. *Tuak*, a palm wine, is served in moderation with sometimes a little *arak* or rice brandy, but for the most part, water is the favoured drink. The aroma of coconut oil, used universally in Bali for cooking purposes, pervades the whole function. Its odour will be noticeable to the visitor at all times.

At home and at work the Balinese like to dress simply in a skirt or *kain*, of batik or handwoven cotton. The women wear their skirts wrapped tightly around the waist, held up by a bright-coloured sash, or *stagen*, and reaching to the ankles. In the villages many of the women go about their daily work bare breasted, but carry a scarf which may be draped loosely over the breasts or wound around them and tied. This is used to cover up when appearing in front of a superior, or entering the temple, or on the approach of strangers and foreigners. There is a trend now towards the more universal use of the Malay blouse, or *kebaja*, a gaily-coloured sleeved garment worn outside the skirt (Plates 4, 40). This is particularly so with the younger people who prefer to enhance and maintain their figures by the use of the brassiere. It seems inevitable that in another generation the picturesque habit of going about bare breasted will have substantially disappeared. The men wear a sarong-type costume extending from the waist to just below the knees, tied in the front or folded to produce a double pleated overlap. The men wear a small square of batik (*udeng*) as a kind of turban wound on the head. Formerly worn with one corner forming a high crest as may be seen in old-style Balinese carvings, the younger generation now prefer smaller, tighter turbans or none at all.

While the everyday dress of the Balinese villager is simple and scant, the dress worn on formal and festival occasions is very elaborate indeed. Many men still appear in elaborate fabric skirts, a rich brocade tied over the breast with a silk scarf, in which the ceremonial *kris* in its wooden or ivory sheath is carried shoulder high. The women are bound from hips to armpits in a long length of glittering cloth, the underskirt finishing in a train passing backwards between the legs and trailing away on the ground behind. Their hair is carefully done, tied at the back, and decorated with a tiara-like crown of flowers such as frangipanni, *tjempaka* and jasmine, carefully built up, fastened in place and clipped to shape. The crown of flowers in the well-to-do may be augmented by ornaments and flowers of gold (Plate 26). The pierced ears, which normally carry small rolls of palm leaf as decoration, are adorned with tapered cylinders of gold, *subeng*, inserted in them. Particularly spectacular are the costumes worn for dancing performances, which will be detailed in a later chapter. Little jewellery is worn, and is limited generally to a bracelet or armband made in black coral, which is said to prevent the development of rheumatic conditions in the joints. The Balinese do not, as a rule, wear necklaces.

Cleanliness is essential to the Balinese. Bathing twice a day is normal, and most evenings both men and women can be seen in the village baths or in the rivers and streams enjoying the cooling and refreshing water. Baths are usually low-walled enclosures with nominal separation of the sexes, where water splashes forth from spouts along the walls under which the bathers stand. It is polite to hide one's genitals from one's fellow bathers by covering them with the hand. A clear skin is desired and admired, and to avoid excessive sunburn the Balinese keep to the shade as much as possible. Various macerated leaves and spices and coconut oil are used to soothe and smooth the skin. The hair is anointed with perfumed coconut oil. Women's hair is worn long in most cases, wound in a bun on the back of the head with a portion of the end of the hair hanging down from it. Most men have now adopted short hair styles, however, and women are tending in the same direction.

Uneven teeth, and particularly long canine teeth, are considered a disfigurement. The long teeth of dogs must be avoided, and so at puberty most people have their teeth filed to level them out and to shorten them if they are too long. If it is not done at this time, it normally forms a part of the wedding ceremony discussed in the next chapter. It is believed that in marriage even teeth prevent dissension, jealousy, argument, anger and other emotions that may disrupt married life.

# 7

# *Childhood and Marriage*

The family is the basic unit in Balinese society. The ties that bind every individual to his family and his family to the community and to the Balinese people as a whole, exert a powerful influence over the beliefs and customs of the people. The family is an eternal and continually expanding social unit binding together the living members and their ancestors. Every Balinese therefore regards it as an important duty to marry an at early age and to raise a family to maintain the line of descent. Furthermore it is only by marriage that a man can enter into the responsible life of the village by becoming a member of the village council, the *krama desa*. In the desire to raise a family a man has a natural preference for male children who will look after him in his old age and who will ensure the performance of adequate cremation rites to liberate his soul for future reincarnation. Family succession is regarded as so important by the Balinese that failure of a wife to have children provides adequate grounds for divorce, or alternatively for a man taking a second wife.

Pregnancy is clearly a welcome condition in a Balinese household and artificial methods of birth control are generally regarded as being in the category of black magic. Pregnancy is free of restrictive or repressive customs and the life of a woman in child is normal. However, she must continually guard against the influence of *leyaks*, or witches, which feed on the blood of pregnant women and consume the entrails of unborn children! These misfortunes are overcome by the use of magic amulets and symbols provided by the priest. Certain rites are also performed at the approach of gestation to ensure easy birth.

At childbirth the woman is assisted by a midwife, or perhaps only by women relatives. Her husband is usually present. She is supported in a reclining position on a new, clean mat, and birth is assisted by massage. The umbilical cord is tied and must be cut by a sharp bamboo knife. The placenta, umbilical cord, blood and afterbirth are buried in front of the *metén* and a bamboo altar is erected over the spot (Plate 23) and offerings made on it. This is continued for a period of up to two years, and such little altars may frequently be seen.

Children are suckled whenever they cry or whenever they seem to incline to suckle, but mother's milk is not considered sufficient to nourish them, and it is supplemented by boiled rice flour or banana from the very first day. After three or four days the mother returns to normal duties.

Children are not allowed to crawl. This is considered to be an animal habit and unclean. They are therefore carried everywhere by their mothers or by their elder sisters, until they are able to walk, although modern Balinese mothers now tend to disregard this requirement. After three birthdays, or sometimes more, children are weaned.

The mother and child are considered to be religiously 'unclean' (*sebel*) for a period of forty-two days after childbirth. At the end of this period they are cleansed and blessed by the *pemangku* in an elaborate ritual and are then treated as ordinary persons. Of course the birth of a freak or an abnormal child brings evil to the community, and formerly the birth of twins of both sexes was regarded as a calamity. Such a birth was regarded in the same light as incest between brother and sister, and it brought the entire village under an evil curse. This could only be overcome by removing the parents and twins to a remote and unpleasant place, usually the cemetery, together with the house in which the twins were born. Here they had to live for forty-two days after which the house was burned and the *metjaru*, or great purification ceremony had to be performed. This was a costly business and generally embarrassed the unfortunate father financially. However tradition was such that the villagers as a whole generally contributed substantially. It is a curious fact however, that the birth of male and female twins among the higher castes was never regarded as a catastrophe, but as a reincarnation in the womb of souls faithfully married in a previous existence. Today, these superstitions are no longer regarded seriously by the common people and the birth of male and female twins no longer disturbs the even tenor of village life.

Children usually wear nothing for the first few years of their lives except perhaps a few protecting amulets to promote healthy development. The first birthday is an occasion for festivities, when the child is again blessed by the priest. A shadow play is an essential element of the rites at this time. The importance of subsequent birthdays diminishes rapidly and most grown people soon lose count of their ages. On his first birthday the child is given his magic name by the priest, but being secret it is soon forgotten. Names usually follow established practice according to the order of birth of the children. The first, second, third and fourth children of Sudras are called respectively *wayan, madé, njoman* and *ktut.* The names are then repeated for subsequent children. Usually a person is known by this name coupled with the name of his father. But his name may change when he himself marries and has children, a somewhat complicated system of nomenclature.

From the time a child can walk he is left to his own devices and the care of other children. He is allowed to move around the village as he pleases. He is never punished physically and is generally treated as an equal by his parents and elders, listening to all their conversations and observing their actions. In this way the child very quickly develops a sense of self-sufficiency. He becomes well-mannered and acquires a seriousness of outlook that is surprisingly mature. Nothing is hidden from him. At an early age he is acquainted with sex and childbirth and it is normal for small boys and girls to smoke. Some schooling is provided, the children learning first in Balinese and later acquiring a knowledge of Bahasa Indonesia. Fathers assist in their education, and they acquire a knowledge of history and mythology from watching plays and puppet shows. The boys assist their fathers in work in the fields and gardens, the girls learn by assisting their mothers to cook, thresh rice, make offerings and weave cloth.

Boys may be seen at what seems an incredibly young age, nonchalantly smoking a cigarette while doing the most intricate carving in stone or wood (Plate 34), or while painting pictures in tempera. Their progressive development from boyhood to manhood is gradual and unnoticed. In the case of girls, however, the first menstruation is an important event, marking the achievement of womanhood, and being celebrated with appropriate ceremony. On menstruation a girl automatically becomes religiously unclean (*sebel*) and must remain in seclusion until the period is over, when she must be purified by the priest. A feast is then given by the family to celebrate the girl's reappearance as an adult woman.

Any woman is considered *sebel* during menstruation, and during this time she is not permitted to enter the temple, to prepare food, to enter the rice granary, or to draw water from the well. She cannot make offerings or take part in festivals. Her husband usually moves to another house and would certainly not sleep with his wife at this time, a custom that seems to derive from the belief that a man touched by menstrual blood becomes bewitched and his will is weakened.

On reaching the age of puberty it is usual for both young men and young women to undergo the ordeal of the teeth-filing ceremony, although in many cases, because of the expense, this is deferred until marriage. The object is to produce upper front teeth which are uniformly even and of reasonable length. Long, narrow, pointed teeth are regarded as belonging to animals and must be avoided. The filing is done by special priests after a ritual involving the use of incantations, drinking holy water, flower throwing and bell ringing, which are said to render the process painless. Filing must of course be done on an auspicious day. The filings are buried alongside the ancestral shrine. It is dangerous to leave any remnants of the human anatomy lying around, because evil spirits and devils are able to reach a person through them.

In the Bali Aga villages young boys and girls while virgin are charged with the care of divine possessions which cannot be handled by impure people. Their purity is jealously guarded by the community in consequence, and sexual

---

Plate 24. In the market at Denpasar.

Plate 25. Djalan Gadja Mada, the main street of Denpasar. The pony carts are widely used as a means of passenger transport.

licence among the young is severely punished. In the ordinary Balinese villages however, boys and girls enjoy more sexual freedom, but nevertheless maintain a high moral standard. Discretion in these matters is essential. Lovers are generally not seen together in public and no man makes advances to a girl in public. Amongst the Sudra, virginity is not regarded as of great importance, but amongst the highest castes it is considered highly desirable.

In general the usual marriageable age for boys is twenty to twenty-five and for girls eighteen to twenty. Young people meet at the market or at festivals and nocturnal theatrical performances where early friendships are made and attraction develops. The Balinese are not romantics. When a man feels strongly about a woman, he desires to sleep with her and says so. If accepted, the affair may develop into marriage. In difficult cases where shyness or indecision may be involved the course of love is assisted by the use of charms and amulets and magic formulae.

Normally a Balinese makes his marriage arrangements directly with the girl of his choice. Only his father and a few close friends, whose help is necessary, will be told of the impending event. On the day agreed between the parties, the man will elope with the girl to the house of a friend, or to another village. Here the honeymoon will be spent in seclusion. Often the prospective groom arranges to 'kidnap' the bride. In this event the bride will first arrange to send her clothes to their intended hiding place. Then, by arrangement, the groom and his friends will kidnap her as she walks on the street, or as she bathes in the river, and with mock resistance and perhaps a nominal fight with her relatives, she will be whisked away to the chosen retreat.

Special offerings are made at the lovers' hiding place, and it is important that the union be consummated before these offerings wilt in order to legalise the arrangement and make

PLATE 26. Part of the ritual of a wedding ceremony—raising hands in the *sembah* of reverence before the family shrine.

PLATE 27. Part of a cremation ceremony at Karangasem showing a small *wadah* in the form of a chair. In this case burial had taken place previously and cremation was of the bones only. These remained at the cemetery and were not carried in the procession.

F

the marriage binding. This is the real marriage bond, made before the gods. Subsequent formal ceremonies are merely confirmation of an event already concluded. The wedding ceremonies must take place within a few days of the kidnapping, but in some cases are delayed for a much longer period until sufficient finance becomes available. Formerly, before the official wedding ceremonies could be held, the relatives of the groom had to negotiate with the bride's father and pay the amount of the 'ransom', the bride purchase money, but this practice has now been discarded almost completely.

There are marriages of arrangement where the parents of the man will request the hand of the daughter of a friend for their son. Such marriages are not uncommon amongst high caste people where this type of arrangement is thought superior to kidnapping. It can be used to ensure a satisfactory marriage with a girl of equal caste. Marriage does not take place in this case until the girl is mature, and no girl can be married in this way against her will, in contradistinction, for example, to the child marriages of India. Premarital intercourse may be permitted in this type of marriage, but since virginity is regarded as of importance among the higher castes, a special defloration ceremony is held followed by verification, bathing, and purification by the priest. The legalisation ceremony is held fifteen days later.

The formal public wedding ceremony and festival must take place on a propitious day. The ceremony is held at the home of the groom's father. Here the guests assemble in their finest clothes, bringing presents for the happy couple. The women congregate together in one part of the compound and the men congregate separately. If the teeth of the bride or bridegroom have not been filed, this ceremony takes place first. The two are first prepared for the ordeal by the priest, a *pedanda*, who recites many magic formulae, rings his little brass bell incessantly, throws flowers in the direction of the couple, sprinkles holy water on them, and finally administers liberal amounts of holy water which are swallowed. It seems possible that some pain-killing ingredients may be introduced at this stage. The patients are then placed on their backs on a bed set up in one of the *balés* of the compound, and the special priest appointed to carry out the tooth filing steps forward. He makes magic signs over the teeth, places a small section of cane between the teeth to prevent the jaws from closing, and to give the patient something to bite on, and with standard files, proceeds to level the upper teeth between the canines. This takes from fifteen to thirty minutes during which the patient has rest periods when he or she rinses away the filings for subsequent burial by the family shrine. After this ceremony the couple sit together and take food.

The marriage ceremony begins with worship before the family shrine, or alternatively a temporary shrine set up for the purpose. The bride and groom, resplendent in formal costumes of colourful woven cloth and wearing ornate head dresses of gold decorated with flowers, together with their attendants, make obeisance before the shrine, raising hands in the *sembah* of reverence (Plate 26). The couple then enter the marriage pavilion and are seated before the white robed priest, who has already performed blessings and purifications with magic recitations in Sanskrit, much sprinkling of holy water, flower flinging and bell ringing. Turning towards the bride and groom he then sanctifies and purifies the union symbolically with food, salt and holy water, placing a mark on the forehead of each to signify protection against evils.

During the formal ceremonies the guests seem to take little notice of the actual proceedings, preferring to chat amongst themselves, to sip coffee and to eat pastry, rice cakes and other delicacies. A *wayang* orchestra plays softly and continuously. A shadow play without a screen, the *wayang lemah*, usually proceeds continuously, and there may be recitations from the *Ardjuna Wiwaha*. When the formal purification ceremony is finished the main banquet is served and the guests settle down to watch plays and dances.

In Bali, marriage between cousins and marriage with divorced women and widows is permissible. There are no restrictions outside those of caste and incest. A man may not normally marry a woman of higher caste than himself. A man may not marry his sister or the daughter of his teacher (who is considered as his father). A woman who marries a foreigner, however, loses the right to her Balinese 'nationality', even though the marriage is permissible. There are signs, how-ever, that these restrictions are not so strictly applied today as they were formerly.

Polygamy is permitted in Bali but its practice is rare nowa-days. The former Radjas had many wives of their own and lower castes, but today few people can offord more than one wife. Normally a wife lives in the home of the man she marries. This may be the paternal home in the case of an eldest son, but otherwise the newly married man must try to obtain a vacant plot of land on which he must first build a temporary family shrine and then a house. When a man takes a second wife she may live in a separate house in the family compound, or she may live in another compound, or even in another village.

Although the man is the head of the family and must represent the family at law and before the council, Balinese women enjoy substantially equal status in the household. Relations between husband and wife are frank and friendly. The man owns the house, the associated rice field, the cattle and implements necessary to work it. The woman owns her clothes and ornaments, the household equipment and the pigs and chickens. Very generally the woman works and earns her own money by weaving and by selling produce at the market. She manages the finances of the family, and at times may be its sole support. She has absolute right to the money she herself has earned.

Divorce is practised by the Balinese and is a simple pro-cedure. A man may divorce his wife on the grounds of adultery, sterility, laziness and neglect, or incompatibility. A woman may divorce her husband on the grounds of impot-ence, cruelty and his inability to support her. A woman wanting a divorce simply leaves her husband's home. The divorce is made final by the village council, which adjudi-cates the case. Formerly the dissolution was confirmed by the breaking of a Chinese *kepeng* symbolising the breaking of the marriage bond, but this custom has now fallen into disuse.

# 8

# *Cremation*

The Balinese believe that the soul is immortal and that the body is merely the vehicle for its containment. When the soul leaves the body and refuses to return in spite of appropriate appeals to the deities, death is considered to have occurred. Nevertheless the soul remains loosely associated with the body and must be released by its obliteration in order to be able to return and be reincarnated into other beings. Bali Aga practice was formerly to dispose of the remains by burial, or by abandonment to the elements and wild animals, as is still practised in some primitive mountain villages such as Trunyan on Lake Batur. The practice of cremation as a more complete release for the soul was introduced into Bali about the thirteenth century and has since become an important element of Balinese life and religion. A rich and complete cremation provides a fitting climax to life, is regarded as a necessary rite, and is very often financed by life savings specifically set aside for the purpose by the deceased. The occasion is therefore a joyous one, not an occasion for mourning. It represents the liberation of the soul for possible reincarnation into a higher status, for which a good life is an essential prerequisite. The souls of the guilty are liable to rebirth as lowly, unpleasant or unclean beings such as snakes and dogs. The spiritual aspects of cremation and reincarnation are thus used to support the social necessity of good and honest citizenship.

On a man's death his relatives assemble at the family house, bringing presents of food. The corpse, placed in one of the pavilions of the house, must await an auspicious day for burial. On that day it is composed, anointed with spices, and the teeth are filed if this has not previously been done. Pieces of mirror are placed on the eyelids, a gold ring with a ruby is placed in the mouth, bits of steel on the teeth,

59

jasmine flowers in the nostrils and iron nails on the limbs. These accoutrements, known as *bantén sutji*, are symbolic of rebirth with enhanced senses, stronger teeth and limbs, brighter eyes and fragrant breath. Finally the body is wrapped in white cloth and placed in a straw mat. It is then taken to the cemetery accompanied by song and music, the relatives bringing offerings and holy water. Burial takes place in very simple graves marked only with stones, bamboo stakes or small shrubs. Simplicity is the keynote because sooner or later the remains will be removed for cremation.

Formerly the body remained in the cemetery for a period of forty-two days, after which cremation could take place, but this custom has now been discarded and cremation can take place at any time after death. Very often cremation is postponed, even for years, until sufficient money becomes available to carry out the rather expensive rite. On the other hand, where there is no financial obstacle, cremation nowadays can be undertaken almost immediately and without burial beforehand.

In any case, as for a burial, cremation must be undertaken only on an auspicious day as determined by the officiating high priest. Before this day relatives open the grave and recover as much of the remains as may be possible. These are returned to the house and placed in the pavilion with the family's prized possessions, covered with cloths and decorated with offerings and other accessories to help the soul along its way. Of these, the most important from the point of view of the ensuing ceremony is the *adegan*, an effigy of the deceased in the traditional palm-leaf *tjili* form. The effigy is taken to the burial ground, where the soul is persuaded to enter it, after which it is blessed in the family shrine and is treated similarly to the corpse, being sprinkled with holy water and equipped with *bantén sutji*. The effigy is placed alongside the remains.

On the eve of the cremation the effigy is taken in procession to the house of the high priest for final blessing, the procession being as grand as possible, with the relatives and the family dressed in their finest clothes, wearing their finest jewellery and *krises*. Orchestras and dancers lead the procession and the women bring offerings. The effigy is carried by a member of the family shaded by an umbrella, and groups of male relations bring up the rear. The effigy is blessed by the priest by sprinkling with holy water and casting flowers with appropriate incantation. The procession then returns to the house, where throughout the night music, dancing, a shadow play and other performances entertain the participants.

Where cremations are undertaken soon after death and without burial, the corpse is prepared in the manner described above for the ordinary funeral. It is finally blessed by the priest and is then ready for the journey to the cremation ground, which is normally the village or town cemetery.

From dawn on the day of cremation there is great activity. The cremation tower and the sarcophagus which have previously been prepared and stored, are brought to the front of the house. At the cremation grounds the bamboo altars and paper roofed earth platform for the actual cremation are finally prepared.

The cremation tower, or *wadah*, is a high structure of wood and bamboo bound together with rattan cane, covered with coloured paper and cotton ornaments, tinsel and small mirrors. The tower is supported on a rectangular grid of bamboo poles carried on the shoulders of up to a hundred men (Plates 27, 29). On this is a wide base, a symbol of the foundation of the world, frequently incorporating the turtle and snake motif. Above it are three platforms, diminishing in size, representing the mountains, with bunches of flowers and leaves on the corners to represent the forests. Above these is an open space called the *balé balean*, formed by four wooden posts, representing the space between heaven and earth. On this platform the body of the dead is placed. Above the *balé balean* is a series of roofs in the style of a pagoda or *meru*, which represents the heavens. There are always an odd number of roofs according to the caste of the deceased—one for Sudras, from three to eleven for the aristocratic castes, and none for the Brahmanic priests for whom an empty chair, or *padmasana*, is substituted (Plate 29). The rear of the tower may be adorned with a very large representation of the head of Bhoma, Son of the Earth, a fanged monster with large extended wings spreading each side of the tower and covered with coloured cotton wool, but nowadays this figure is generally omitted. The tower is served by a bamboo bridge or by a simple bamboo ladder which enables the *balé balean* to be reached from the ground.

The sarcophagus, or coffin, is shaped according to the caste of the deceased. Sudras burn their dead in open cases shaped to represent *gadjamina*, a mythical animal, half elephant half fish. Formerly Brahmanas were burned in coffins shaped like a bull for men and a cow for women, Satrias in a coffin shaped like a *singhasari* or winged lion, and Wesias in a coffin shaped like a deer. Today most aristocratic castes who can afford to do so, use the bull and the cow. The coffins are carved in wood, a hollow tree trunk being used for the body, the back of which opens as a lid. They are covered with coloured fabrics and ornamented with gilding, the colours again being dictated by caste (Plate 28).

After the guests have eaten the village *kulkul* is beaten to signal the beginning of the march to the cremation ground. Holy water is sprinkled to clear the way to the tower of evil spirits, and the body is brought from the house over the wall, avoiding the main gate if possible. It is immediately snatched by others, a mock fight ensuing, during which the corpse is moved about violently so that its sense of direction is destroyed and it can never find its way back to the house. Finally it is carried up the bridge or ladder and placed on the *balé balean* of the cremation tower and the procession to the cremation grounds proceeds.

Usually the procession is led by two small boys as standard bearers followed by men and women gaily dressed in colourful costumes bearing offerings on their heads. These are followed by men bearing the sarcophagus on a bamboo platform, women carrying the effigies, if any, the dancers and musicians and finally the men bearing the cremation tower. The tower bearers follow an erratic and unpredictable path, rotating and tilting the tower in order further to confuse evil spirits and further to mislead the dead. At every crossroads the tower is rotated three times. It is led by a long rope tied to the *balé balean* at one end and held by relatives at the other (Plate 29).

The noisy and erratic procession finally reaches the cremation ground where the coffin is placed on the cremation mound. A canopy of white cloth is stretched over it and relatives walk three times round the mound as a mark of respect. Two small chickens, symbolic of the flight of the soul, which had been tied to the tower, are released. The body is brought down from the platform by the bridge or ladder and is led by the women attendants to the coffin and placed inside. Relatives crowd round to have a last look at the body which is exposed to view by cutting its bindings. The high priest then mounts the platform, gives prayers and anoints the body with holy water brought by relatives and friends. The *adegan* and other important accessories are placed on the body, the lid of the coffin is replaced and the offerings are placed under and around it. After a final blessing the priest sets fire to the pile.

The orchestras play louder than ever. The spectators plunder the tower for its decorations before it too is set on fire. The noise and excitement is intense. The coffin is consumed (Plate 30) and the funeral pyre is kept massed together to ensure calcination, after which water is poured over the fire. The remaining bits of bone and some ash, now distinguished from the wood ashes by being white as distinct from black, are piled together, covered with palm leaves, and surrounded by white cotton cloth as a symbol of completion and finality. The remaining ashes are blessed and placed in an urn made of a yellow coconut. This coconut is then dressed with white cloth, a coloured apron, flowers and pieces of palm leaf to form still another effigy of the deceased. At sundown the remaining ashes and this effigy are escorted to the sea or a nearby river which flows into the sea, where they are strewn over the water, after which the spectators bathe before returning home.

The provision of the necessary impedimenta for a cremation of this kind is a relatively expensive matter, and amongst ordinary people it is sometimes customary to hold a collective cremation ceremony for a number of dead at the one time. Thus there may be one or more towers involved in the procession, each transporting a number of bodies, and there will then be a number of coffins fired together. In these circumstances the spectacle is most impressive and is accompanied by the smell of smoke and burning flesh coupled with the odour peculiar to concentrated humanity. In multiple cremations it is important that dead of the same caste are carried in the tower appropriate to them.

Of course there are also cremations based on the same principles, but of the very simplest kind to meet the needs of those who cannot afford a considerable spectacle, even on a communal basis. In these cases the procedure most commonly adopted is to dispense with a sarcophagus or coffin. The body, wrapped in white cloth and woven matting and equipped with *bantén sutji*, is carried to the cemetery on a simple bier. This consists of the *balé balean* only, that is, a simple platform covered by a simple single roof supported from it on four short posts. The bier is usually decorated with paper and coloured cottons and carries, as well as the body, some offerings and personal possessions. A rectangular framework is erected nearby made of the green trunks of banana trees, which will not burn. The body is supported within this framework and a fire is lit beneath it. Some two to three hours is necessary to complete a cremation carried out in this way (Plate 31) and the task is undertaken by the men. They poke and prod the body to promote incineration and even comminute the more difficult portions to ensure complete destruction. The whole process is closely watched by the women and children present and an orchestra provides an appropriate musical background. After the body is entirely consumed the ashes are washed with water to distinguish the bones and bone-ash from the ashes of the fire. The bones are then collected, washed clean and assembled in the form of a human body as an effigy of the deceased, and some are placed in a yellow coconut which is also dressed in effigy. The final services of the priest are then employed to bless the remains which are taken at sundown to the sea or a nearby river for dispersal.

Payment for the priest's services is always in kind, but is graded according to the family's financial circumstances, the services being very similar but differing in the quality and effectiveness of the priest's incantations.

Cremations are quite frequently held somewhere or other on the island and those interested in the colourful ceremonies and customs of the Balinese should not miss any opportunity of seeing one. The opportunity to see a full scale cremation with tower and sarcophagus, however, does not often occur. Such cremations are today confined to a relatively small number of people of wealth and high caste. The simple ceremony which has just been described is the one held in the vast majority of cases and is the one that will be seen most frequently by visitors.

In former times the notorious Indian custom of suttee was practised in Bali—that is the sacrifice of widows of princes and noblemen by burning alive on the funeral pyres of their husbands. At times also, mass consumption by fire of an aristocrat's low-caste wives, followers and servants at his cremation ceremony was also indulged in. These practices were, however, falling into disuse when the Dutch put an end to them at the beginning of this century.

At times a simple cremation ceremony is held in a cemetery when only a few relatives are present and when only a small effigy of the deceased is burnt. This is done in cases where a relative has died in a place remote from the home of his people, who must nevertheless ensure, in this way, the proper and complete liberation of the soul of the deceased so that it may be free to return to the family's ancestral shrine.

The completion of the cremation ceremony itself does not discharge all the obligations of the deceased's relatives. The soul of the departed must now be consecrated by further ceremonies of a similar nature, after which it becomes deified and can be allotted a resting place in the family temple where a shrine may be erected for the purpose. After cremation the soul is consulted through a medium to enquire whether the cremation was successful and if all is well. Its ties with earth are then finally broken by the symbolic smashing of egg shells. Forty-two days after cremation the *mukur* takes place. This is a ceremony designed to ensure for the soul the attainment of the highest heaven allotted to it by caste, and dispensation for minor sins. A second bier decorated with white and gold is constructed. The same priest is engaged. The same guests are invited. The same accessories are made. New effigies identical with the *adegans* made for the actual cremation, are blessed and purified by the priest and then burned. The ashes are placed in a yellow coconut shell, wrapped in white cloth and decorated with flowers as an image of the dead person. This is the *sekah*, symbolic of the spirit of the deceased. It is placed on the white and gold bier and again a procession moves to the sea with the same reckless abandon and erratic movement as in the cremation ceremony itself. Here the *sekah* is placed on a boat, taken far enough out to sea so that it will not return, and thrown to the waters. The bier is again destroyed by fire together with all the accessories, after which the participants bathe at the water's edge before returning home happy in the knowledge that they have now completed their obligations to their dead. Purification by earth, fire and water has ensured continuing guidance by them as deities just as in life they fostered and protected their families.

# 9

# *Industry and Agriculture*

There is very little industry in the true sense of the word in Bali. With one exception there are no factories producing manufactured goods. The government firm Patal operates a cotton spinning mill at Tohpati. The government also operates a small but quite modern weaving plant, Balitex, at Tjelangu. Both are in the Kesiman area close to Denpasar on the main road to the east. Patal Tohpati produces only undyed yarn and Balitex produces only cloth in the grey or in a very small range of plain colours. Dyeing of cotton yarn is still largely a cottage industry and dyed yarns can frequently be seen laid out in the sun to dry along the roadside approaching Gianjar. These yarns are supplied to small weavers who produce small quantities of cloth in gay and sometimes complicated patterns.

At the port of Benoa salt is extracted from sea water for domestic use. Here tidal ponds produce a regular supply of salt-rich sand which is collected in crude wooden troughs. By passing water slowly through the sand a concentrated solution is obtained which is then evaporated to dryness in forty-gallon drums cut longitudinally and heated over a fire fed with coconut husks, sticks, leaves and other rubbish. The whole process is crude in the extreme, but is suited to the economy of the country. Another salt-making village is Kusamba on the southeast coast opposite the Goa Lawah, the bat cave. Here the final product is obtained by solar evaporation in shallow wooden trays, but the salt water is all carried manually up a steep black sand beach to the sand beds where it is concentrated!

Brick, tile and pottery making may perhaps be regarded as industries although always undertaken on a small scale in any one area. A brickworks is generally established where the soil has a sufficient proportion of clay for the purpose.

Bricks made from the clay pug are formed on the ground in removable wooden gang moulds and are then sun-dried for one or two days. They are then stacked to form a furnace in themselves in which a timber fire is lit. The whole structure is covered by a thatched roof to give protection from rain and to provide shade for the workers. Firing continues for three days during which smoke issues freely through and around the thatched roof—an incongruous sight to see. When the bricks are burnt the whole furnace is dismantled and the bricks delivered to consumers. The bricks are small in size, twenty-five by twelve by four centimetres. As a result of the very light burning they receive the bricks are of a delightful warm, deep pink shade and are extremely soft. The visitor who comes across workmen building in brick and stone should stop and inspect the work. Bricks are laid in conjunction with the soft volcanic siltstone of the island, which will be carved with intricate designs after construction work has been concluded. Bricks and stone inserts are fitted together very closely with only a thin smear of cement mortar between them, giving a most attractive appearance. To achieve this, bricks must be of an accuracy impossible to obtain in any other way than by shaping to exact size. This is done by planing the bricks with a simple tool in essence identical with a wooden carpenter's plane, the softness of the brick and stone making this possible.

Roofing tiles are very often made in association with bricks, the general techniques being similar. Flat rectangular slabs of clay pug are formed in shallow wooden moulds and placed on a wooden former shaped in the form of a barrel tile. The clay is pressed to the shape of the former, the edges trimmed and supported by short lengths of split bamboo. The shaped tile thus supported is then rested in an almost vertical position against drying racks set up in a long wide thatched shed in which the eaves of the roof very nearly reach the ground. By shading the tiles in this way and reducing the flow of air round them, the rate of drying is retarded and the tiles harden up without cracking. The dried tiles are then stacked in a simple brick furnace and fired by wood fire.

Pottery making is predominantly a cottage industry, although very often groups of pottery makers will be found in one village. The pots are thrown by hand on a wooden wheel which is rotated by hand. When the clay pug is formed to the desired shape it is sun-dried and fired in the open using rice straw as a fuel. The finished pots are usually taken to market for sale by the women who carry them piled high over their heads.

With these few exceptions the industry of the island is almost exclusively agricultural, and agricultural production is almost exclusively of rice. There are, of course, the village gardens where tropical fruit trees grow naturally and in profusion and where vegetables, sweet potato and corn are grown. In the highland districts unirrigated terraces are used for growing fodder crops of various kinds, beans, tapioca, cassava and *kendal* trees whose leaves are used for cattle feed. But the great bulk of the country is used for rice growing, and wherever land is not required for villages and wherever it can be irrigated by water led from mountain streams, it is terraced and divided into small individual plots known as *sawah*. These plots are levelled and surrounded by embankments of grass-covered sod which serve to hold the water in the *sawah* itself, and to retain the soil between successive levels of the rice terraces (Plate 2). In many cases also, water is conducted from terrace to terrace along these retaining walls in special channels cut in them for the purpose.

The whole Balinese landscape is dominated by the rice terraces, which extend up the faces of steep slopes in the deeply-cut lowland valleys, and ascend the hills and mountains in an endless succession of steps until they can go no higher. Water is led from rivers and streams through channels, rock tunnels and bamboo pipes to the highest terraces, and overflows into successively lower terraces until it can be used no more and must be returned to some stream or watercourse for redeployment elsewhere.

The Balinese are able to cultivate two successive crops of rice each year, as well as an intermediate crop, which provides a natural rotation and nitrogen enrichment. Intermediate crops such as tobacco, chillis, soy beans and so on are used. As soon as a crop is harvested the ground is prepared by ploughing with a crude wooden single-tined plough drawn by Balinese cows. The ground is ploughed and harrowed over and over again to reduce weed growth and to incorporate the weeds and the rice stubble from the previous crop into the soil.

Seed for replanting is selected from amongst the finest ears of the preceding crop. It is soaked and sprinkled with water until it sprouts and is then transferred to a nursery plot in the corner of the field on a propitious day according to the calendar. After about six weeks the young stools are planted out in the *sawah* after suitable offerings have been made to Dewi Sri, the goddess of agriculture and fertility, wife of Wisnu. The owner of the *sawah* first plants nine stools, beginning with a central one, then placing one at each of the cardinal points, north, east, south and west in that order, remembering that the Balinese 'north' is towards the big mountain, Gunung Agung. The last four are placed again in clockwise order between the first four. This represents the eight-pointed star, a magic symbol of some consequence in Balinese symbolic rites. The rest of the seedlings are then planted in regular rows one hand span apart. From then on they must be well watered, weeded and carefully tended. Offerings must be made to protect the growing rice from the depredations of insects and caterpillars. After forty-two days more offerings are made to celebrate its feast day. After some twelve weeks the heads begin to appear, when the rice is said to be pregnant. More offerings are then made and a full growth is assured by bringing to the field a palm-leaf figure of a woman, a *tjili*, with male genitals. Not long after this the water is drained from the field and the rice ripens quickly while the ground hardens sufficiently to enable harvesting to proceed.

---

PLATE 28. The coffin in the form of a cow, ridden by a young relative of the deceased, is carried to the cremation ground supported on the shoulders of the men, whose erratic course is designed to confuse the soul of the dead.

PLATE 29. The cremation procession of a Brahmana priestess. The *wadah* is in the form of a *padmasana*. A young relative and the officiating priest ride with the body to the cemetery. The *wadah* is carried on the shoulders of many men who proceed in an erratic fashion. Note the rope by which the relatives lead the body along the way.

With the fullness of the grain sometimes comes the menace of birds and mice. The *sawah* is covered with strings hung with dangling objects, put in motion to scare the birds as required by a small boy who keeps continuous watch. Scarecrows are erected but are of limited value. Mice are caught and killed when they become troublesome. This is a critical period and fully occupies the time of the men and boys of the village.

It is not unusual at any season to see adjacent fields and terraces containing new plantings or half-grown crops, in close juxtaposition to newly-tilled fields or fields of ripe grain ready for harvesting. The newly planted *sawah* have an ethereal appearance, the sky being mirrored in the shallow water which covers them, and provide a marked contrast to the dense, lush, viridian stand of growing crops and the bright yellow masses of dried straw and ripened heads. The picture is an entrancing one and the sight of the never-ending paddy fields rising in terrace after terrace is a continuous delight.

The Balinese system of irrigation is of ancient origin and has been developed, modified and improved over many centuries. Since water supply from rivers is common property and since any one unit of the irrigation system will serve a number of villagers, or a number of villages, or even whole districts, the development and operation of the system requires community cooperation. This led to the establishment of *subaks*, which are, in effect, cooperative agricultural societies in the nature of local water boards. The *subaks* are composed of all members owning *sawah* in a common irrigation area, who are compelled to join. They elect their own leader and operating committee from their own number. Every member of the *subak* must carry out its instructions.

---

PLATE 30. Incineration of the coffin at a cremation ceremony. The coffin has been opened and the body placed within it together with offerings and personal possessions. Kindling has been piled below it and the fire is well under way.

PLATE 31. Cremation of the lower castes. Ordinarily a coffin is not involved. The body is consumed by a fire confined within the walls of a structure formed of green banana trunks. The men attend to the fire while the women sit to one side and chat.

F

Meetings are generally held in a temple compound located in the rice fields, which belongs to the *subak* and is dedicated to agricultural deities (Plates 45, 46). Many such temples will be seen by the visitor, often of elaborate style. Here the *subak* determines work to be done in repairing, maintaining and improving the terraces themselves, the walls and embankments, the water supply system and the rostering of irrigation. Here the committee apportions the work to be done to the various members, reports on its relations with the officials of neighbouring *subaks* and other authorities, and accounts for the finances of the *subak* itself. Meetings are often followed by a social gathering or a banquet.

There are rules governing the operation of *subaks* which are designed to ensure an equitable distribution of available rice lands. A man who for some reason has acquired more land than he himself can work, is requested to share the produce with others appointed to help him. All members abide by the rules and by the decisions of the committee and the whole work of the cooperative is carried on in a spirit of complete and harmonious communal unity.

When the grain is ripe and ready for harvest small offerings are made at the corner of the field to keep evil spirits away and an effigy of the goddess of rice, known as a *dewa nini*, is made using a small sheaf of rice heads tied together in the form of a woman's skirt. The *dewa nini* is tied to a stick which is placed in the ground near the main irrigation inlet. Harvesting can then proceed.

In Bali the men prepare the fields, plant the rice and tend it to maturity. But at harvest time, men, women and children all help. Because they are in the sun and lack their customary shade, all rice harvesters wear cloth coats and large basket-work hats with domed tops. A line of reapers, perhaps forty or fifty strong, starts at one side of the *sawah* and moves slowly but steadily across it (Plate 32). The stalks are gathered one by one in the left hand and cut off at a standard length below the ear by pressing against a short blade mounted in a wooden handle held in the palm of the right hand. The successive severed stalks are then held in the right hand to form a small bundle. At intervals these are taken by assistants, assembled together and tied in sheaves, each of which weighs from thirty to forty pounds. These sheaves are carried to the family granary as is the custom, by the men two at a time on heavy shoulder poles, by the women singly on their heads. Harvesting is cooperative and proceeds from *sawah* to *sawah*. When it is completed, the effigies of the rice goddess in each *sawah* are dressed by adding a head dress made of the stalks embellished with pieces of palm leaf and flowers formed in the shape of a fan. These are carried to the village and placed in the granaries of the individual *sawah* owners and left there untouched until eaten by rats. Under no circumstances would a Balinese eat the rice contained in a rice goddess effigy.

Just as the distribution of labour in the rice field is done strictly according to custom, so it is in other fields of industry. In general, all heavy work requiring much physical effort such as agriculture and building work is allotted to men. In addition men are traditionally the tradesmen and artists, carvers, and painters, writers and musicians. No woman would dream of painting a picture or carving a statue. On the other hand, women raise pigs and chickens, sell wares in the market, transport materials, cook in the home, prepare rice and fetch water. In addition they may be seen laying bricks and doing roadwork. Offerings are normally made by the women.

Children from an early age, as we have seen, assist their parents in their daily tasks. The boys weed in the rice fields and tend the ducks and cows. If their father is a cratfsman they learn his craft. It is not unusual to see small boys of ten or twelve busily carving the most intricate patterns in stone (Plate 34), or carving traditional wooden figures. The girls help their mothers in their domestic duties, learn to cook and to weave and to deal in the market. The Balinese believe that a woman who is unable to cook and to weave is a sinner.

Labour amongst the Balinese is not often paid for in cash, but is generally exchanged for the labour of another. The communal village system with cooperative working of the land ensures that nearly everybody shares in the general prosperity. If one man requires a house built, another, skilled in that work, will do it. As a recompense the owner will perform some service for the builder which his own skills make possible. By the exchange of labour and produce in this way Balinese villagers can live happily even though modestly, without the necessity for much actual money. However in the larger towns this cooperative barter system gives way more and more to a system of monetary exchange, increasing with the size of the town and with the progressive introduction of a wider range of imported manufactured goods. It seems inevitable that as the desire for more products of this sort increases, the exchange of goods on a monetary basis will ultimately predominate. One of the difficulties associated with this change is the comparative inability of the Balinese to produce goods for export to exchange for manufactured imports. Probably the most prolific source of income in the immediate future is by serving the needs and interests of visiting tourists and by the production of pictures and carvings for sale to them. In these fields the Balinese remain supreme, and the development of their art and dance forms is discussed in the remaining chapters of this section.

# 10

## *Balinese Art*

Artistry is ingrained in the Balinese. Irrespective of their way of life, their social status, their knowledge and training, most Balinese men are accomplished in either painting, carving, sculpture, music or the dramatic arts. It is quite astonishing how often a visit to a simple villager's home reveals a competent painter at work. His morning has probably been spent in his *sawah* attending to his rice crop. His afternoon will be spent on most careful and exacting work on a painting of high quality and sensitivity. It is surprising how often an obscure and unpretentious village will be found to have a famous orchestra, or be able to stage dancing of top quality, and how often the gay, vivacious little girl attending a tiny food stall at the village market by day, becomes the elegantly-dressed, bejewelled and graceful dancer in the evening.

Art seems to be ingrained in the population and they have a natural aptitude for it. Nevertheless certain arts are the prerogative of one or other of the sexes. Painting, sculpture and orchestral playing are arts strictly reserved for men. The women excel at weaving, temple decoration, preparation of offerings and the making of *lamaks* and *tjilis*. Both men and women, however, perform in the traditional dances of the island, although even here, some are reserved exclusively for men and some are exclusively for women.

A natural urge for self-expression combined with a life providing an abundance of leisure time, promoted artistic pursuits amongst the Balinese. Their art developed along both primitive and sophisticated lines because its practice was never confined as the prerogative of an intellectual class. Thus today, the finest musicians, artists and sculptors may be found in all classes of society from the lowest to the highest.

The early artist in Bali did not paint or carve or produce stone sculpture for the intrinsic value of the product. There was always a purpose in mind. Carving in stone was done for the purpose of constructing a temple gate, or making a temple guardian or for some other similar utilitarian purpose. Painting was done with the idea of conveying a story, or producing a decorative curtain, and so on. Carving in wood was done for the purpose of decorating a house pavilion, or a pair of doors, or producing carved figures with a religious purpose, such as *artjas*, or to decorate musical instruments. This work was generally done without remuneration other than some reciprocal service or gift. It was not until the 1930's that Balinese artists began to turn out pictures and wood carvings for sale to an increasing body of tourists and to supply the demand for this work overseas. This circumstance had a profound effect on Balinese art styles, and the subsequent post-war development of tourism has continued to influence them. There is little doubt but that this influence will have an accelerated effect in the 1970's, and will probably result in the prostitution of a refined and graceful art form and of the present advanced level of craftsmanship.

We know very little of the ancient arts of the Balinese. In tropical climates little other than stone endures over the centuries, and in Bali even the stone used for carvings and monuments is soft and relatively friable. Some minor examples of archaic art have been found, but essentially the oldest relics and monuments that still exist belong to the period when the kings of Pedjeng and Bedulu reigned and when Bali had broken free from Java in the eleventh century after the death of Erlangga, the part-Balinese king of Kahuripan, in central Java. It is in the area around these two districts that these monuments can be seen. They show the influence of the classical style of India which the Hindus introduced into Java, and which flourished there in the eighth and ninth centuries when the great temples of Borobudur and Prambanan were built. At this time architectural style and artistic embellishment were dominated by religious concepts and traditions, but with the decline of the classical influence after the time of Erlangga, the Hindu and Buddhist religious domination in art forms disappeared and the earthy, animistic approach of the Balinese emerged once more. A similar trend developed in the east Javanese kingdom of

Madjapahit, where a characteristic folk art replaced classical Indian styles. Bali became a dependency of Madjapahit in the fourteenth century and the trend away from classical forms in Balinese art was accelerated as a consequence. This trend toward naturalism, in decorative work in particular, was taken much further in Bali than it was in Java, and was responsible for the elaborate and imaginative decoration that the visitor sees all around him in the temples, shrines and houses today.

Relics of the classical period of Balinese art are greatly valued and are carefully guarded in the temples of some of the remote villages. Amongst them are the famous stone altar at Batukandik in the small island of Nusa Penida, and the largest statue in Bali, that of Dewa Ratu Pantjering Djagat kept unseen except by the virgin boys who clean it periodically, in a *meru* in the village temple of Trunyan, an old village on the eastern shore of Lake Batur. A unique antiquity is the great bronze drum kept in the Pura Panataram Sasih in Pedjeng. This drum is of Chinese form, elongated, with four handles, and is of large size, but the decorative motifs cast on it are not Chinese and the drum is thought to be perhaps of Javanese origin.

At Gunung Kawi near Tampaksiring in the cliffs forming the sides of the deeply-cut valley of the Pakrisan River, are nine monuments in the shape of ancient burial towers or *tjandi*, carved into the vertical rock face. Nearby are rectangular niches cut in the same cliffs which are believed to have been used to expose corpses to decay and wild animals as was the custom of the day. These monuments are known as the 'King's Tombs' (Plate 43) and are thought to have been the burial place of Erlangga's brother, King Anak Wungsu, who ruled Bali in his name whilst he was absent in Kahuripan.

A statue of Mahendradatta, Erlangga's mother in the form of the goddess Giri Putri, also belonging to the classical period of Balinese art, is in the sanctuary of Bukit Darma in Kutri near Bedulu. In the same locality is the famous 'Elephant Cave', a small cavern containing an image of Ganesa together with two *linggas*, known as Goa Gadja. The mouth of the cave is carved in the form of the head of an enormous fat monster splitting open the rock with his hands (Plate 41). This cavern faces a terrace on which there is a sunken bath (Plate 42) with carved stone figures holding water pots from which water spouts issue forth. It is thought to date from the eighth century. There are other less important antiquities in stone, but the number is limited.

Today sculpture in stone is done almost exclusively for the decoration of temples, public buildings and the houses of the wealthy. The visitor to Bali is immediately struck with the number of these decorations and their extent and intricacy. They are based fundamentally on certain mythical and religious figures which have become stylised and embellished with intricate tracery based on the natural form of certain vines, shrubs and flowers. At times it is difficult to discern the basic figure in the design, for example the beak and eye of Garuda formalised into corner ornaments frequently found on temple gates, *karang tjuring*. At others the stylised figure is easily discernible, for example the monstrous face with bulging eyes, prominent canine teeth, hanging tongue and long fingernails which appears over the gates of temples and palaces, *karang tjewiri* (Plates 7, 16). Another design derived from it is *karang bintulu* in which the teeth are surmounted by a single bulging eye and the representation of a mountain. In other cases the derivation of the design is clearly shown, the carving being of a completely natural nature, such as is seen in the pediments of the columns supporting the roof of the Kerta Gosa, the courthouse at Klungkung, which are carved in the realistic forms of animals (Plate 49). And finally there are endless numbers of decorative statues of demons and guardians which normally stand outside the gates of temples or at many crossroads and road junctions. These are of human form but with exaggerated features, prominent eyes and teeth and a wealth of lavish decorative detail.

The only stone available in Bali for carving is a soft volcanic siltstone of very fine grain quarried from the beds of the rivers which cut deeply into the volcanic terrain. When first cut out in blocks of suitable size the stone can be roughly shaped with adzes. It is then transported to its final location and put in position in its ultimate resting place.

Final shaping and detailed carving are carried out *in situ*. Where wall decoration is required the same system applies. Blocks of this soft stone are incorporated in the brick structure and are subsequently carved to form the required decoration, whether it be in the form of simple undecorated stylised shapes, or with rich, flowery, intricate embellishment. The exception is the production of free-standing figures and statuettes which are carved in workshops or under the shade of trees and awnings on the roadside. Youngsters carving such demoniacal figures may be seen at any time in the stone-carving shops at Tegaltamu on the road between Denpasar and Ubud (Plate 34).

Architectural design as such is unknown in Bali. The sculptors superintend the construction of a temple, direct the size, shape and placement of the stones, and do the carving. The design emerges from the sculptor's mind without formal drawings or plans, and the remarkable part of it all is that there are literally thousands of ordinary Balinese who have the talent to do this.

The art of wood carving was similarly confined in early times to the decoration of houses and pavilions by carving pillars and beams in similar intricate patterns based on floral motives and on figures both real and legendary. It was not until the 1930's that the carving of wooden figures as individual decorative objects became popular. With an increase in tourism the enterprising Balinese found a ready market for their skills and rapidly developed a typical Balinese style of carved wood figures. A beautiful dark-red, close-grained wood, *sawo*, was used in the main. Carved figures were representative of Balinese life and customs, men and women in formal costumes, dancers, drummers and so on. These were carved at first with great realism and great intricacy of detail and were polished by burnishing with bamboo. With growing demand for export, however, the quality inevitably deteriorated. The rows of Djanger dancers seen in curio shops all over the world will be familiar to all. Other and inferior woods came into use and the polish and finish declined. Good carvings of this period are of great interest as historical relics of a rapidly disappearing art form. The pause in demand consequent upon the second world war was fortunate in that the prostitution of a fine art ceased, or was at least delayed.

The development of the wood carver's art in Bali in the post-war era has been to continue the development of a naturalistic trend in a more sophisticated and modern style. In many cases the figures became exaggerated by elongating bodies, arms and legs, producing a distinctive and attractive style, except where this distortion is excessive. This tendency is still present but seems to be becoming more restrained. Modern carvings are still representative of the people, their customs and their traditional dress, but both figures and dress have become simplified. The intricate carving has disappeared in favour of smoother surfaces and a more delicate silhouette. The use of ebony, both black, and grained in delightful shades of black and brown, is increasing. The old method of bamboo burnishing has disappeared in favour of a fine glasspaper finish subsequently wax polished.

Again it seems axiomatic that almost any Balinese can carve in wood. There are thousands of competent carvers, both young and old. They work always with delicate steel carving tools and use a light wooden mallet. The wood block is first roughly shaped by hand axe and then carved resting it against a wooden block for support, holding the piece firm by means of the toes, and working in a squatting position. That such fine work can be produced under such apparently uncomfortable circumstances has to be seen to be believed. Men and boys can be seen at all times carving figures (both for polishing and for painting), panels and screens, squatting in the shade of open pavilions and shelters in the carving shops of Mas.

There is no doubt that with the development of international jet travel through Bali, the demand for carvings in wood and ivory will increase. A greater output will be required to meet this demand. This will inevitably lead to lower standards of workmanship. It is to be hoped that in part at least, the Balinese will continue to produce first class carvings (for which it will be necessary to charge appropriate prices) and maintain their reputation as the world's finest craftsmen in wood.

Early painting in Bali was confined to the decoration of

curtains and hangings, usually with mythical motifs or astrological calendars. Good examples are to be seen in the museum at Denpasar. Astrological calendars were typified by a series of squares, each filled by an appropriate scene, including gods, devils and princes, one for each of the thirty-five days of the Balinese month. Very crude modern imitations are made today. The acquisition of a good authentic example is difficult. In genuine examples the paintings are stylised according to the rule of custom. All spaces between figures are filled with background designs to suggest an appropriate environment. Successive scenes are separated by formal drawings of mountains or forests. Battle scenes are crowded with bodies, weapons and arrows. Faces are nearly always three-quarter, never in profile. Gods and heroes are depicted in graceful attitudes, with long thin limbs, normal eyes and teeth and delicate hands. Demons and devils have thick and hairy bodies (repulsive to the Balinese), bulging eyes, long pointed teeth and are usually depicted in a dark colour. All wear elaborate costumes.

These early paintings were made with a palette restricted to five colours—red, blue, yellow, black and white—a fairly normal range among primitive artists, being based on natural earths and materials normally available. However, there was a renaissance in the art of painting in the 1930's when increasing contact with the outside world widened the range of colours available, and the Balinese began to paint pictures depicting events in their daily life. Pictures representative of the markets, rice growing, village activities, cremation and so on, were now produced by the young artists around Ubud, but these pictures nevertheless retained something of the formal rules previously applicable to calendar painting. Canvases are completely covered in detail. Details are formally drawn. Dress and figure position are conventional. But the colours have become more subtle and light and shade have been introduced by colour gradation and highlights, although perspective, as known in the west, is not apparent even today in the characteristic Balinese painting.

Again the second world war was probably instrumental in allowing this art form to develop properly before it became over-commercialised. Today in Bali, and particularly around

Ubud, there are some hundreds of painters. As in all countries a large number are incompetent and their work is crude, inartistic and cheap. But there is a hard core of very accomplished Balinese artists who, with the encouragement of indigenous entrepreneurs and teachers and of a handful of European artists who have settled in the community, are producing excellent works in this characteristic Balinese style (Plate 33). It behoves visitors to be selective in their purchases of paintings and to look for quality rather than price if, as in the case of wood carving, the skill and artistry of the Balinese is to be maintained at a high level and encouraged to improve. Already there is evidence of the change from tempera painting on glazed cotton cloth to oil painting on prepared canvas, and of the gradual adoption of a more western style of painting with perspective of both form and colour. At present, however, there is a tendency to continue the Balinese habit of repetition of scenic formulae rather than to produce individual unrelated compositions, and to paint nude and semi-nude figures with exaggerated bosoms in the belief no doubt that these will appeal to the erotic sense of the tourist-buyer.

While paintings and sculpture are the leading art forms in Bali, there are others of considerable importance to the community which might be classified more as crafts than as arts. A great deal of intricate and delicate silver ware is made. The work and the products can always be seen at Tjeluk and in the silver shops at Klungkung. Metal working probably reaches its zenith in the production of the traditional *kris*. The blade of the *kris* is either straight, or more often sinuous, since it is thought to have been derived originally from the form of *naga*, the mythical snake, the body forming the blade and the head the handle. Blades are built up by beating together alternate layers of meteoritic nickel and iron, with subsequent etching to produce the Damascene-like patterns of silver and black. The sheaths are normally made of wood or ivory. The handles are shaped in a variety of forms and materials, the best samples being of beaten gold, studded with rubies and other gems. The blacksmith is an important man in any village, and although of low caste is addressed in the high language when working with his tools. The blacksmith works in his family compound at a crude smithy fed with charcoal, the fire being blown by a fan generally home made out of bamboo and wood. The *kris* is an object of some reverence in Bali, is essential with formal dress, and is said to be possessed with the spirit of its owner. The quality is regarded as a mark of the owner's importance. There are many legends concerning the magic prowess of the *kris*.

Among the artistic activities of the women, we have already discussed the preparation of offerings of food and fruit in the form of highly decorative arrangements set upon special trays, carried to the temples on their heads. We have also mentioned the crafts of home weaving as practised by the women and the patterns produced by the Balinese art of *ikat*, or pattern dyeing in warp and weft before weaving, which produces a soft and diffuse effect. There is one further activity normally carried out by the women, however, that must be mentioned because of its importance in communal life and in national decoration. This is the making of *lamaks* and *tjilis*. The former are long strips made up of palm leaf pinned together with bamboo slivers. They are some twelve to eighteen inches wide and of various lengths up to some twenty feet. They are used as decoration at temple feasts, to hang on shrines and altars at appropriate ceremonies, and to hang at the entrances to family compounds at Galunggan and other national festival times (Plate 35). They are decorated with a variety of designs cut out of palm leaves of contrasting colour pinned to the background. Usually the decorative motifs are in green attached to a background of yellow. They are very attractive, but their life is limited as the fresh leaves soon wilt in the heat.

Amongst the decorative patterns applied to *lamaks* none is more characteristic than the *tjili*. This is a stylised figure similar to the rice goddess (*dewa nini*) and is representative of Dewi Sri, the goddess of fertility and beauty and of Melanting, the goddess of the market. The shape takes the form of a body represented by a skirt, with arms and hands, surmouted by a fan-shaped head dress, and there are usually representations of eyes, ear rings or breasts. There are very many forms of *tjilis* (Fig. 4, Plate 35) which vary from

4. Some typical *tjili* designs.

village to village, and some have become so stylised as to be hardly recognisable as such. They are used not only to decorate the *lamaks*, but also as individual offerings of symbolic nature, and in completely stylised forms as decorative motifs in clay and stone. The visitor to Bali will see many examples of both *lamaks* and *tjilis*, particularly during the holy days Galunggan and Kuninggan.

# 11

# *Drama, Music and the Dance*

The music of Bali is exclusively orchestral although there are orchestras of various types and sizes suited to the musical needs of every occasion. These orchestras are essentially percussive in nature consisting in the main of *gongs*, drums and xylophones. The *gongs* are the basic instruments required to play the deepest notes. They vary in size, the largest *gongs* being some four feet in diameter in the form of a bronze dish suspended vertically from an elaborately carved, gilded wooden frame and struck on a protruberance formed in the centre. Large *gongs* are very costly, come from Java and are difficult to obtain.

Associated with the *gongs* are sets of bronze 'bells' in the same general form, but suspended horizontally in sets of thirteen (*reyong*) or ten (*trompong*). These are played by three muscians who kneel before them and who strike the 'bells' with wooden rods partially bound with cord with which they can produce either sharp or muted notes as required. Melodies and chords are played on these instruments.

The drums are usually two in number. They are double-ended with diaphragms tuned to different notes. One is larger than the other one. One is said to be male, the other female. They are called *kendang* and are played with the palms of the hands and the fingers. They provide the basic rhythm and accent of the music. They are played by the most knowledgeable of the musicians, one of whom is generally the leader of the orchestra and arranges and composes much of the orchestra's music.

The xylophone-like instruments provide the real music, the musical themes and variations, the main outline of each composition. They have bronze keys which are struck with a wooden mallet. Below the keys a series of tuned hollow bamboo resonators enhance and magnify the sound. The notes are muted by the player's left hand after having been struck by the mallet held in the right hand. The whole instrument is mounted in a magnificently carved wooden frame, and is played by the performer sitting cross-legged on the stage in front of it. There are various types and sizes of these xylophone-like instruments, *gangsa*, depending on the range of notes included, and there is one type, the *gendér*, which has ten notes and is played with both hands. These instruments together make up the basic *gamelan* orchestra, but may be augmented by cymbals and bamboo flutes if desired.

The music produced by a *gamelan* orchestra is immediately acceptable to western ears, and one's first experience of a performance is an exciting and emotional occasion. The octave is divided into five intervals and the character of the music is therefore quite different to that of occidental music of the normal kind. Also, because of its orchestral character, the interplay of instruments and melodies, the multiplicity of harmonious sounds, it has no suggestion of the ethereal and discordant plaintiveness of purely eastern music. The general effect is a metallic one, although this can be accentuated enormously in loud passages or almost eliminated in soft passages at the will of the players. The whole effect can be varied almost instantaneously from one of sweetness and charm to one of strong and martial character, from a gentle tinkling of sound to a crashing crescendo, from delicate melody to a harsh discordant chord. The music has a recognised musical form, generally starting with a solo introduction, followed by the main theme and concluding with variations on it. No music is used. Everyone plays from memory. The timing is perfection itself, the result of long and patient practice repeated until each player 'has the music in his belly'. Although the orchestra has a leader his effect is not apparent to the listener and seems to confirm

---

PLATE 32. Reaping the rice crop, a community undertaking.

PLATE 33. A Balinese painter at work. The scenes painted are typical of Balinese village life and are executed in tempera.

the suggestion that a conductor is not really necessary to a good orchestra.

Every village, almost every *bandjar*, has an orchestra. The village owns the instruments, which are very costly. The instruments for a full *gamelan* orchestra will cost at least $US 7,500. The performers are drawn from the villagers, and practice is usually held in the *balé bandjar* or at some other central location, such as a *puri* if one is available. The performers are therefore drawn from all walks of life. While it is required of an aristocrat to learn to perform music, it is the prerogative of all ordinary Balinese. In the orchestra a prince is no different to a peasant. Caste does not count, and all performers sit at the same level on the stage while playing. The musicians are not paid for their services, but are usually feasted by the audience. If any money is given them it is used for the furtherance of the orchestra itself, perhaps being applied to paying off the instruments. At every Balinese feast or festival, wedding, cremation or birthday, an orchestra is essential. On these occasions the musicians give their services freely in return for food and hospitality.

The *gendér wayang* is a small group composed of from two to four *gendér* which is used to accompany the shadow plays. Played with both hands and with a somewhat different scale from the normal *gangsa* it provides music of a more liquid nature suited to accompany the recitation of the *wayang* performer. The notes of the *gendér* are produced by striking pieces of bamboo which are integral with their bamboo resonators and are suspended in line by cords from a carved wooden frame. *Gendér* music is used as a background on any occasion. It is pleasant and acceptable because of its soft, smooth, melodious and rippling character.

Music is, of course, basic to the dance. All formal Balinese dances are accompanied by an orchestra of some kind, a

---

PLATE 34. Rock carvers at work in the shade of trees by the roadside at Tegaltamu. Much of the work is done by very young boys.

PLATE 35. A typical *lamak* made of yellow and green palm leaf pinned together with bamboo slivers. Note the formalised tree at the top which represents the mountain and the *tjili* design in the centre (lower left).

PLATE 36. Modern wood carvings by the master, Ida Bagus Njana, show the future trend in Balinese wood carving style (lower right).

G

kind best suited to the particular performance. As well as supporting an orchestra, every village supports a group of dancers chosen from amongst its members. Whereas orchestras are composed solely of male performers, the dancers are drawn from both sexes. Training commences when the dancers are from six to eight years old. They are chosen for their potential talent, fitness and personality as far as it can be judged at that age. A former distinguished dancer usually acts as teacher. He commences by teaching the dancers the elementary movements which appear in most of the formal dances. These are repeated under guidance until they are instinctive in the learners. Training for any one dance form goes on for months. It is coupled with physical exercise designed to promote suppleness and good physical condition. Such is the physical demand on the performer that most dancers retire at the age of fifteen or sixteen, but this is not universally so and there are many fine dancers of middle age, both men and women.

The village society of dancers must also acquire the intricate and gorgeous costumes to clothe the dancers, who are presented for their first public appearance on an auspicious date after suitable offerings have been made. The dancers, like musicians, are not paid, but are recompensed with feasts and food. When money is given it goes to the society, perhaps to pay for costumes. Annually a day is given over to making offerings to all theatrical costumes, masks, puppets and musical instruments. On this day (*tumpek wayang*) theatrical societies all over the island hold feasts, but no performance of any kind is allowed.

Balinese dancing is a sophisticated stylised form of entertainment in which every movement has a studied purpose and is in harmony with every other movement. Elements of classical Javanese dancing have been combined with the primitive magic rituals and naturalism of the Balinese. The recognised dance forms are theatrical in character and normally tell a story based on the Ramayana or on factual or mythical historical episodes of the past, rather than provide a pure interpretation of the music alone. The stories generally involve the machinations of witches, the trials and tribulations of princes, episodes of love and hate, peace and war, and inevitably, the eternal fight between good and evil.

The size of the audience is the best evidence of its appreciation. A successful performer and a successful performance will attract a big crowd, the people coming from villages at a considerable distance. Every night there will be a performance of the dance in a number of villages. Some become noted for the quality of their dances, and particularly for the standard of performance of particular forms. Thus the Barong Dance as performed in the villages of Batubulan and Singapadu is considered probably the best example of this form. The Ketjak Dance as performed at Peliatan is well-regarded. This is not to say, however that the quality of these dances as performed elsewhere is not of a very high standard indeed.

There are formalities of dress and there are formal recognised movements which are basic to the Balinese dance. These are perhaps epitomised in the Legong Dance. Here the attitudes of the body, and in particular the positions of the arms and hands are of great importance, particularly the latter. The characteristic eastern attitude of the fingers, fully extended and curved backwards to a remarkable degree, is maintained at all times. The fan is clasped in the palm of the right hand and pressed against the forearm, moved but little and then only with a sudden, jerky movement. The dancer never smiles and maintains a serious expression at all times. The eyes, however, are used to develop expression. They are held wide open, rolled from side to side, and their movements are accompanied by sudden rapid movements of the head to one side, accompanied by shaking the shoulders in a fluttering gesture of pleasure. There are some eighteen standard attitudes involved in *legong* dancing, which is the finest, most classical, traditional dance form of the Balinese. It is exclusive to girls, two of whom usually perform together and move in conjunction. The costumes worn are rich and elegant. They consist of a wrapped skirt held in place by a binding of cloth which extends from the hips to the armpits and is tied by a sash of gilt cloth. A vest of tooled and gilt leather hangs over the shoulders. There is a collar set with jewels and mirrors. The front of the skirt hangs in a train which passes backwards between the legs. It is particularly fascinating to watch the *legong* dancer sweep this train aside with her foot when moving backwards or making a turning motion so that it will not impede or interfere with her dance steps. The whole is surmounted by a magnificent head dress built up in front over the forehead in the shape of a tiara. It is formed of fresh flowers of frangipanni tied together and clipped to shape. Golden ear plugs (*subang*), armbands and a fan complete the picture (Plate 38).

The Legong Dance is a pure classical form designed to interpret the music which it accompanies by enacting a story taken from the mythical Malat. Here the two *legongs* represent Prince Lasem and Princess Rangkesari. The Prince has forcibly abducted the Princess, but she resists his advances. On learning of the impending approach of her betrothed, the Crown Prince of Kahuripan, she begs Prince Lasem to set her free and so avoid a fight. He refuses and goes out to meet Kahuripan. On the way he encounters a raven, a bird of ill omen, but taking no heed of this warning he chases the bird away and proceeds to fight Kahuripan, who kills him in the fight that ensues. The dancers enact the various characters in the story by their motions only, the text being recited by a storyteller while the dancing proceeds.

*Legong* dancing, always performed by two girls, enters into many other theatrical-type dances as a part of the proceedings, very often as an introductory episode. In the modified form, the *djogéd*, it is used at feasts and gatherings to entice male members of the audience to dance with the *legong* who 'flirts' with selected partners with her eyes. The man must endeavour to approach the dancer near enough to feel the warmth of her skin and to smell the odour of her perfume, the Balinese equivalent of kissing.

The Baris Dance is a part of the ritual enacted at feasts in the older villages. It is a stately war dance in which a dozen warriors with a characteristic head dress in white cloth with

PLATE 37. The *barong*, a mythical animal which is the main attraction in the Barong Dance. With teeth bared he prepares to attack a witch in the form of a Rangda.

PLATE 38. *Legong* dancers in a typical pose characteristic of *legong* dancing showing the elegant costumes worn and the elaborate head dress made of frangipanni flowers.

a high peak at the rear and bedecked with red flowers at the front, dance in two rows. They carry spears tipped with peacock feathers and banded in silver and black. It is accompanied by a *gamelan gong*. The music starts quietly, the dancers striking heroic poses, but as the dance proceeds the music grows more menacing, the pace quickens, and the dancers work themselves up into a frenzy. With shouts of defiance each dancer draws his *kris* and a series of stylised duel ensues, the dance ending with the defeat of one of the characters.

The traditional Baris Dance is very rarely seen today. The modern version is performed by a single dancer who wears a dress similar to the traditional dress (Plate 39) but he does not carry the traditional spear. The white triangular head dress sits well down over the brow. The cloak, formed of multicoloured strips of fabric hanging from the yoke, is bulky and sits high on the shoulders. Short red leggings complete the ensemble. The whole effect is characteristic and gives an impression of a short, thickset, somewhat stilted individual. The dance itself cannot of course terminate in a fight, but it is nevertheless based on traditional lines, gradually working up to a climax of frenzied movement and dramatic poses symbolic of a warrior preparing for battle.

The Kebiyar Dance is today generally incorporated in a *legong* performance. It was introduced to Bali by the famous dancer I Maria. This dance is done with the body only, the dancer sitting on the stage. He is dressed in a brocade wrapped around his body like a skirt and binding him from the waist upward. The binding is fastened by a gilt sash. One end trails on the ground. He wears a small cloth turban embellished by a large hibiscus blossom mounted on springs. In his right hand he carries a fan. The whole dance is charged with intensity. The music starts with a resounding opening chord. The dancer is startled and galvanised into life. His eyes dilate. His head, arms and hands dart about,

---

PLATE 39. A Baris dancer in a pose of defiance. The elaborate and colourful costume made up of a number of strips of highly-coloured material, together with the triangular white hat, is traditional.

PLATE 40. Young women carrying offerings in a religious procession.

while his body sways from side to side and quivers with excitement. The dance works up to a climax, then becomes quiet and sensuous, only to become electric again, and this alternation of peace and agitation continues throughout. In the modern version the dancer performs before a *trompong*, or set of gongs, on which he plays from time to time in unison with the orchestra. Thus a *kebiyar* performer must be an accomplished musician as well as a remarkably competent dancer.

A short dance frequently seen as part of a *legong* performance is the Oleg Tambulilingan. This is a dance depicting a flirtation between two bumble bees while seeking honey among the flowers in a flower garden. The dancers imitate the action of flying by holding the ends of sashes in each hand and waving their arms in graceful undulations. Wooden figures of *legong* dancers, their fabric 'wings' draped gracefully from their hands, are frequently seen in the carving shops of Mas.

The Djauk is a short dance accompanied by a *pelegongan* orchestra and is performed by a masked dancer in the form of a *raksasa*. It represents the sinister movements of a typical demon which the dancer's mask portrays.

The Topeng Tua is another short dance of classical character. It is performed by a masked dancer whose mask is a representation of a white-faced old man. The steps of the dance are slow and deliberate and portray the unsteady movements of an elderly person. The accompanying *gong* music is appropriate to the movements. The dance ends with a stately bow from the dancer executed with the simulated difficulty that an old man would have after the exhausting effort of the dance. It is a rewarding experience to witness this simple dance when performed by a skilled and artistic person.

There are several forms of drama which involve dancing, singing and rhetoric which are performed with orchestral accompaniment. The stories are concerned with the Mahabrata and Ramayana epics, mythical characters and stories such as those of the Ardjuna Wiwaha, the Malat, and episodes in Balinese history. In most cases the dancers wear masks indicative of the characters they represent. The Mask

Dance, or *prembon*, normally seen today, is based on the story of the King Sri Krisna Kapakisan and his subjugation of a number of his disloyal subjects by virtue of the magic of a special, sacred *kris* given to him by Gadja Mada, Prime Minister of Madjapahit. The dialogue and dancing are accompanied by a *pelegongan* orchestra. Another similar dance is the Kupu Kupu Tjarum based on the story of Prince Bimaniu, whose deep and reverent meditation overcame the attacks of the jealous consorts of a number of beautiful nymphs who fell in love with him. This dance is remarkable for the fact that the chief character, the prince himself, remains motionless throughout almost the whole of the performance.

The Djanger Dance is a popular form of entertainment and is one in which a certain amount of *ad hoc* latitude is permitted. The dance is performed by twelve girls and twelve boys. The girls divide into two groups facing each other from opposite sides of a square. The boys divide similarly into two groups facing one another on the other two sides of the square. The leader sits on a mat in the centre. The girls wear a distinctive head dress in the form of a tooled leather tiara extended with paper flowers. Their dresses are of gold with tooled leather collars and belts. The boys wear a velvet vest over their white shirts. The dances, accompanied by flute, *gong* and drums, are less bound by tradition than other Balinese dances, are varied in character and include singing, chanting, comic sketches and even acrobatics.

One of the most unique, spectacular and frequently performed dances today is the Ketjak Dance. One of the finest performances is to be seen in Peliatan where the stage is the forecourt of the village temple, the main gate of which forms a background to the spectacle. The dance is always held after dark and is illuminated only by a small group of oil lamps burning in the centre of the arena. The dance is unique in that there is no orchestral accompaniment.

The players are few in number and enact the familiar episode of the Ramayana in which Sita accompanies Rama to the forest where he pursues the golden deer. Sita is kidnapped by Rawana, king of the demons, but is able to inform Rama of her plight by virtue of the good offices of Hanuman. Rama is attacked by Meganada, the son of Rawana, who shoots him with an arrow which turns into a snake and entwines itself around Rama immobilising him. Rama calls his ally, Garuda, to help him and Garuda destroys the snake by pecking it. Sugriwa, the king of the monkeys, then takes up the fight on Rama's behalf and he and his army of monkeys attack Meganada and his army of demons. The fight that ensues forms the climax of the dance. Sugriwa overcomes Meganada and Rama is reunited with his wife Sita.

The players are accompanied by a male chorus numbering some one hundred members. The men are clad only in a short sarong in a large black and white check pattern (*saput poleng*). Over the right ear they wear a red flower, over the left ear a white one. The dance commences with the entry of the chorus through the temple gate chanting continuously '*ketjak ketjak ketjak ketjak*', combined with other occasional shouts and calls. The chorus takes up positions squatting in radial rows around the circumference of the stage area leaving only a small circular space in the centre surrounding the lamp standard. Here the principal dancers perform. During the whole of the dance, which usually lasts for an hour, the chorus keeps up a continual chant—'*ketjak ketjak ketjak ketjak*'. The men bounce up and down on their heels while swaying from side to side in time with the chant with occasional shaking of the shoulders. As the play proceeds the chorus enters into the action by reaching forward with hands outstretched, by lying back on the haunches, by advancing towards the actors and retreating from them again. As the climax is reached the men of the chorus divide into two sections, one supporting the demons, one supporting the monkeys. Advancing and receding as the fight proceeds the men become the chief feature of the dance, which proceeds to an exciting climax with the triumph of the monkey king.

The combination of the unusual character of the Ketjak Dance with its continual chanted accompaniment and its gradual crescendo of excitement, and the atmosphere created by the weak flickering of a few oil lamps surrounded by the warmth and soft darkness of the tropic night, produces an effect full of magic into which the spectators are inevitably drawn.

The Barong Dance, as a pure spectacle, is probably the modern Balinese dance most appreciated by the visitor. It is generally performed early in the morning with a temple background. This is the proper setting for all Balinese dances. The performers enter and retire through the elegant and decorative gateway of the temple, introducing themselves to the audience by slowly descending the few steps from the gate down to the temple forecourt.

The *barong* is a mythical animal in the general form of a Chinese lion, called *barong ket* (Plate 37). It is manipulated by two men, one of whom takes the head and one of whom takes the tail. The body, which stretches between them at some length and with an attractive sag, is covered with long white hair and is surmounted by a series of tooled leather saddles. Those over the buttocks and the shoulders are the largest and the most ornate. A high, arched tail is decorated with gold and covered with small pieces of mirror. The head is a ferocious wooden mask with bulging eyes, long canine teeth and a hinged lower jaw. This is manipulated with great effect by the performer at the front and makes a fine snapping noise when the mouth is suddenly closed. The head mask is surmounted by an upstanding gilded collar decorated with two red pompoms.

The Barong Dance is accompanied by a full *pelegongan* orchestra and commences with a prelude which has nothing to do with the succeeding play but serves to introduce the *barong* and provides an opportunity for considerable comedy. The *barong* enters first, and with sinuous motions, snapping jaws and wagging tail descends the steps from the temple gate to the arena, where it continues its amusing antics. The *barong's* friend the monkey then appears, followed by three men wearing masks. These are palm-wine tappers. They are after the *barong* who has killed a child belonging to one of them. They attack the *barong* but the monkey intervenes and bites off the nose of one of the men, after which they retire from the fight. This prelude is then followed by a short *legong* dance by two girls in the typical costume of the *legong* dancer.

The play proper then begins with the entry of two man-
servants of the Queen, Dewi Kunti. They are the narrators
of the play. They explain that their beloved Prince Sadewa
is to be sacrificed that day to Betari Durga, goddess of death.
While they are discussing the distasteful prospect, a witch
who is a disciple of Betari Durga appears. After the witch
leaves, the menservants, Punta and Widjil, ask the Prime
Minister for his help. The Prime Minister appears, followed
closely by the Queen, Dewi Kunti, a servant and Prince
Sadewa. The Queen is despondent at the impending disaster
which seems bound to overtake her son. The witch, fearing
the Queen may refuse to sacrifice her son after all, bewitches
Dewi Kunti, who beats Sadewa and then orders the Prime
Minister to take him to the cemetery where Betari Durga
lives. The Prime Minister being reluctant to do so, the
witch returns and in turn bewitches him so that he turns
on Sadewa and ties him to a tree in front of Betari Durga's
home.

While Sadewa is awaiting his fate tied to the tree, Siwa
appears in the form of a priest. Taking pity on Sadewa, he
gives him immortality. Shortly after this Betari Durga arrives
on the shoulders of her followers. She takes the form of a
Rangda, a fearsome witch with long white hair reaching to
her knees, a hideous face with bulging eyes and prominent
teeth, a long tongue, sagging breasts and long fingernails on
both hands. She makes strenuous efforts to kill and consume
Sadewa, but because of his newly-acquired immortality, she
is unsuccessful. Realising her defeat she then asks Sadewa
for redemption. He agrees and kills the Rangda who is then
released from her bondage and returns to heaven once more
as Siwa's wife.

Betari Durga has a disciple named Kalika. She also wishes
to be redeemed, but Sadewa refuses, and they fight. Kalika
uses her magic power and transforms herself into a boar.
The boar is defeated. She reappears as a bird, but is again
defeated. She then reappears as a Rangda, who is much too
powerful for Sadewa to cope with. He enlists the aid of the
*barong*, who fights with the Rangda (Plate 37). The *barong*
calls on the aid of his followers, the *kris* dancers. They
attack the Rangda but are unable to subdue her. In anger

they turn their *krises* on themselves. This is a powerful moment in the play. The *kris* dancers press their weapons against their chests with considerable force and great realism. They tend to become entranced and have generally to be disarmed before doing themselves harm. The play finishes with the sacrifice of a small chicken whose blood must be spilled on the ground, and the *pemangku* sprinkles holy water on the *kris* dancers.

The whole play revolves, like so many Balinese dramatic performances, around the eternal struggle between good and evil. This is a never ending struggle, one in which there is no final decision for either side. The *kris* dancers in the Barong Play, turning their weapons on themselves in despair at the interminable nature of the fight, are the climactic symbol of the eternal conflict.

Spectacular and outstanding performances of the Barong Dance are given weekly at the village temples at Batubulan and at Singapadu. No visitor to Bali should miss seeing a performance.

In contrast, the Barong Landong is a gentle dance of quite different character. It is a dance performed by giant puppets, and has a religious significance. The puppets represent an old woman (*djéro lúh*) with typical protruding forehead and jaw, and a black giant (*djéro gedé*) with an animal face and prominent teeth. They are carried by the dancers who look out from eyeholes cut in the puppets at waist level. The dance is accompanied by a small orchestra of gongs and flutes. There are occasions when the Barong Landong is used as a religious rite to dispel the evil influences under which a village may fall and which cause misfortunes such as sickness among the villagers, or a series of adverse occurrences of any sort. On these occasions the dance is performed at various points throughout the village in order to cleanse it of such troubles. To witness such a performance being enacted in the village street in the quiet of an early evening is to see the Barong Landong at its best, and to feel a sense of real magic and deep emotion.

To conclude this account, mention must be made of what are probably the dramatic presentations most beloved of the Balinese. These are the *wayang* performances. They are based on the stories of the Mahabrata and the Ramayana and are concerned with the deeds of princes reincarnated to save the world by carrying on the eternal fight against evil. These stories were rewritten by the Javanese in Kawi, the 'classical' language. There are two types of *wayang* performance, the *wayang kulit*, or shadow play in which the actors are puppets, and the *wayang wong* in which the performance is given by men dressed in costumes and wearing masks appropriate to the characters.

The puppets used in the *wayang kulit* are stamped out of buffalo-hide parchment and are painted. Each has moveable arms with bamboo sticks attached for manipulation, and a fixed bamboo stick by means of which the puppet can be fixed upright by inserting it into a green banana trunk placed in front of the calico screen for that purpose. The shadows of the puppets are thrown onto this calico screen by an oil lamp behind them over the head of the performer, or *dalang*. The *dalang* manipulates the puppets and at the same time provides the dialogue. The performance is accompanied by the quiet music of a *gendér wayang* and by rhythmic tapping on the box which contains the puppets.

Very often visitors will see two men carrying a large wooden box between them, walking along the roadside. They are taking the puppets to a nearby village for a *wayang kulit* show. The performance generally lasts from two to three hours, and sometimes may continue from midnight until dawn. At the beginning, a representation of a tree, symbolic of the mountains, the *kekajonan*, dances across the stage and then comes to rest in the centre. The characters are then introduced individually and the good characters are placed to the right and the evil characters to the left. The puppets are then removed and the play begins. The characters need no subsequent introduction. They are well known by their

PLATE 41. The elaborately carved entrance to the 'Elephant Cave' at Bedulu. The hands of the monster can be seen splitting the rock open. The surrounding decoration contains many representations of animals and human figures.

PLATE 42. The sunken bath and springs at the site of the 'Elephant Cave' at Bedulu. The water issues from the spouts of water pots held by the carved figures. Note the division into areas for men and women.

shapes and by their 'voices' as interpreted by the *dalang*. Every move is symbolic. The plays are concerned either with the rescue of Sita from the giant Rawana by Rama, assisted by the army of monkeys and their General, Hanuman, or with the deeds of the five Pandawas (one of whom was Ardjuna) and their cousins the Korawas in their fight between the forces of good and evil. But in addition to the traditional characters of the epic, the Balinese have invented characters of their own. These are Parekan, Twalén, and Merdah, who are good, and Delám and Sangut, who are evil. They fight by magic means. Twalén always wins. The antics of these characters and the bawdy dialogue which accompanies them, provide the fun for the Balinese, who remain spellbound throughout the performance, but in the absence of understanding, it becomes boring to the western mind. The play concludes with the replacement of the *kekajonan* in the centre of the stage. The performance of the *wayang kulit* is an essential at children's anniversaries, tooth filing ceremonies, weddings and certain temple feasts.

The *wayang wong* is a performance of the same stories by male dancers who speak the individual parts. They wear costumes and masks which bear the same characteristics as do the puppets representing the same characters in the *wayang kulit*. The performance is accompanied by a *gendér wayang*. Performances of the *wayang wong* are rare today but may sometimes be seen on the occasion of national festivals such as Kuninggan.

The reader will by now have realised the way in which the religious beliefs of the Balinese are basic to their life and culture. The myths of India, handed down through the medium of the Hindu religion, provide the basis for most dramatic performances and for most of the traditional dance forms. An understanding of the broad nature of these myths is essential to the understanding of Balinese dances and of

---

PLATE 43. The 'King's Tombs' near Tampaksiring. Carved in the side of a cliff, the mausoleums take the form of ancient burial towers.

PLATE 44. Shrines in the sanctuary area at the holy spring of Tirta Empul. Thatched with black *idjuk* fibre, these are the most colourful shrines to be seen in Bali.

the Balinese people themselves. Visitors to the island should ensure that they see as many of these dances as they are able to. By this means their understanding of many of the daily habits of the Balinese will be enriched.

# 12

# *Denpasar*

Denpasar is the capital of the Province of Bali and is the centre of regional administration by a Governor representing the Government of the Republic of Indonesia, and an elected Provincial Parliament. It is served by an international airport at Tuban, the runway of which has now been extended to the full extent of the coral reef located at its west (*see map at the end of this volume*). It is also served by the port of Benoa where a causeway extends out into the bay under the protection of Turtle Island. Here small inter-island boats of up to 1,000 tons displacement can berth after negotiating the somewhat narrow and tortuous opening in the encircling coral (see map). At the beginning of the causeway the primitive salt works already described can be inspected.

Denpasar is the centre of military establishments in the island. It has a four hundred bed hospital. The advanced educational requirements of the island are served by a small university with some two thousand students and which conducts courses in Arts, Economics, Agriculture, Animal Husbandry and Medicine.

The main points of interest in Denpasar are the museum, the newly-emerging Temple of Bali, the Bali Art Foundation, the former prince's palace—the Puri Pemetjutan, the market and two interesting and decorative *kulkul* towers. Some detailed notes on these features follow. Their location can be seen by reference to Fig. 5 in which the town plan of central Denpasar is shown.

THE MUSEUM OF DENPASAR

The museum of Denpasar is unpretentious, but contains a very carefully selected collection of items representative of early Balinese life and culture. The quality of the exhibits is undeniably good, and they are well presented. A visit to the museum is a useful preliminary to exploration of the island and its villages. A second visit at a later stage will be found very informative. A visit at some time is a must for every visitor.

The museum is located at Djalan Major Wisnu and faces the open grassy square in the centre of the town known as Tanah Lapang Puputan Badung. It is built in the form of a typical Balinese temple in the soft red brick of the island combined with carved grey stonework. A tall 'split' gate forms the front entrance to an outer court with a watch tower to the left and a gateway on the right leading to the elaborately-carved stone *kulkul* tower just outside it. This *kulkul* tower is of four tiers, the three lower ones being decorated with eight guardians (*raksasas*) on each one. A single drum hangs from the roof.

From the outer courtyard a magnificently carved main gateway, a *padu raksa*, leads over a set of stone steps to the inner courtyard where the main museum building is located. Observe especially the beautifully carved wooden doors of the *padu raksa*, the carved wooden over-lintel, and the excellent carved panels decorating the *aling aling* wall immediately behind it. A smaller gateway to one side, also fitted with beautifully carved wooden doors, provides an easier access to the inner court for the visitor.

The main museum building faces the inner court and is of brick and carved stone. There is a raised covered platform across the front with carved wooden pillars supporting the roof, which is thatched with sago-palm fibre. The front wall of the museum proper has three doors and four window openings fitted with delicately-carved wooden doors and shutters. The outer platform serves as a display area for a

PLATE 45. The inner door, *padu raksa*, to the sanctuary of the *subak* Temple of Bedji at Sangsit in northern Bali. This doorway is typical of the 'rococo' style and over-ornamentation of the temples of the north.

PLATE 46. The unusual *gedong pesimpangan* and associated shrines at the Temple of Bedji. Note the approach to the shrines up a series of four flights of steps each entered by a split gateway, or *tjandi bentar*.

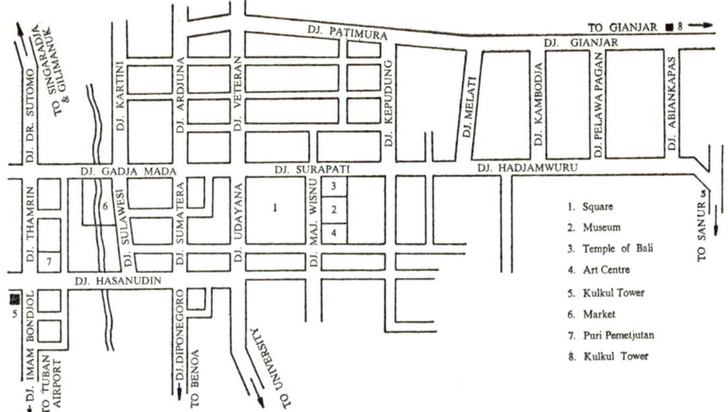

5. Street plan of central Denpasar. 1, Square. 2, Museum. 3, Temple of Bali. 4, Bali Art Foundation. 5, *Kulkul* tower. 6, Market. 7, Puri Pemetjutan. 8, *Kulkul* tower.

number of stone statues, and in the courtyard lies a pair of beautiful bronze cannons in the form of *naga* heads.

The erection of such an elaborate representation of traditional Balinese temple construction may at first sight seem to be extravagantly superfluous in a museum building. It has been done deliberately, however, so that the building and its surroundings form an outdoor exhibit of architectural significance in themselves.

The main building is devoted to exhibits of the arts and crafts of the early Balinese and to early artefacts. Here are to be seen stone-age axes and adzes and other tools as well as their counterparts of the bronze age. There are examples of metalwork in silver and gold, pottery, textiles, early painting, kepeng dolls, palm-leaf and straw *tjilis*, and a variety of early wood carvings both utilitarian and purely artistic. Typical amongst the wood carvings are those representing

---

PLATE 47. The *merus* of Pura Tjandikuning extending out into Lake Bratan. The appearance is enhanced on a misty day when the clouds descend low over the mountains surrounding the lake.

PLATE 48. Lava flowing south from Mt. Agung in the 1963 eruption engulfed this brick gateway to a residence in Gelgel. The houses associated with it and hundreds of others nearby were burnt. The village temple in the background escaped destruction.

H

Wisnu riding on Garuda and Rawana riding Wilmana. Both are subjects frequently seen in carvings produced today. Outstanding is the large wooden figure of Wrehaspati, one of the seven heavenly seers. This figure stands immediately inside the central doorway and is a mass of intricate detail splendidly carved.

An item of great interest is the exhibit demonstrating the mode of writing on strips of *lontar*-palm leaf, which were then assembled together and secured by a cord passing through a central hole in each successive strip, to make books. These early books, written in ancient Balinese or in Sanskrit and often illustrated with drawings, are frequently offered for sale by mendicants. They are generally incomplete and are frequently modern copies of genuine antique examples.

A gateway from the inner court leads to a second building of brick with a typical carved Balinese house-door at the entrance. Here are exhibits of musical instruments, masks, weapons, puppets, woven fabrics and some very intricate and beautiful wood carvings taken from old Balinese buildings. Of particular interest are an old Balinese 'violin', a two-stringed instrument played with a horse-hair bow; *grinsing* and *songket* woven fabrics done by the unique Balinese method of pattern-dying before weaving, or *ikat*; and several *kris* with representations of the snake, *naga*, embossed along the sides of the wavy blades with the head embossed near the handles. The last named specimens seem to confirm the suggestion that the wavy nature of the blade of the *kris* was originally based on a *naga* theme.

THE TEMPLE OF BALI

Adjoining the museum and to the right of it, facing the square, a large new temple complex is at present under construction. When completed this will be the temple for the whole island, the *Pura Djagatnatha*. The great *padmasana*, or throne for the supreme god, surmounted by his chair, built in white coral rock, is almost complete, as is also one minor shrine. The *padmasana* is surrounded by a moat and is approached across a carved stone bridge on each of its four sides. It will be some time before this temple is completed, and it is typical of the Balinese that this work is proceeding while urgently-needed roads and bridges are neglected.

BALI ART FOUNDATION

Adjoining the museum and on the left of it facing the square, is a new art school centre and the Bali Art Foundation (Jajasan Keradjinan Bali). The building itself is set back under the shade of the trees. The verandah along the front is supported by carved wooden posts. Entry is between the piers of a wide 'split' gateway leading to the main door of brick with carved stone. Just inside the main doorway is a wall (*aling aling*) which is elaborately carved. The front window openings are equipped with splendidly carved wooden shutters.

The display consists of modern wood carvings of all types and of modern Balinese paintings. Both of these are representative of a wide range of artists and carvers, whose exhibited work is for sale at fixed prices. The foundation is run by the government for the benefit of Balinese art and artists. It is an exhibition place and a merchandising outlet for their work. Its aim is also to encourage the arts of Bali to flourish.

Amongst the exhibits of contemporary work are some older examples of wood carving, shrine and temple doors, which are not for sale. As an introduction to Balinese carving and painting a visit to the foundation is valuable, and as an introduction to realistic price levels it is informative.

THE PURI PEMETJUTAN

The Palace of the former Radja of Badung is located on the corner of Djalan Hasanudin and Djalan Thamrin (see Fig. 5, station 7). It was built in 1907 to replace the former palace which was destroyed by the Dutch when they overthrew the Radja in 1906 and finally assumed control of the whole of Bali.

The Puri Pemetjutan is probably the best example of a former palace that remains today. It is well kept, and although regarded in the nature of a museum piece, the fact that it is occupied and lived in makes it a place of character and life. A number of young artists paint and exhibit in the various *balés*. One building is given over to orchestral and dancing practice. *Ikat* weaving can be seen here. Fig. 6 shows the layout of the Puri and its component parts.

The main entrance is by a 'split' gate, a *tjandi bentar*, from Djalan Thamrin into a forecourt (A) used for dancing and similar purposes during festivals. From here a gate leads to the second court (B) in which there are two main buildings, the *balé lantang* (C) used for musical practice and for exhibiting paintings, and the *Balairung* (D), a building formerly used for audiences with the Prince and for the reception of royal visitors. Here on the porch, a full *gamelan* orchestra composed of antique pieces is exhibited. The *Balairung* itself is a highly decorated and ornate building as befits its importance.

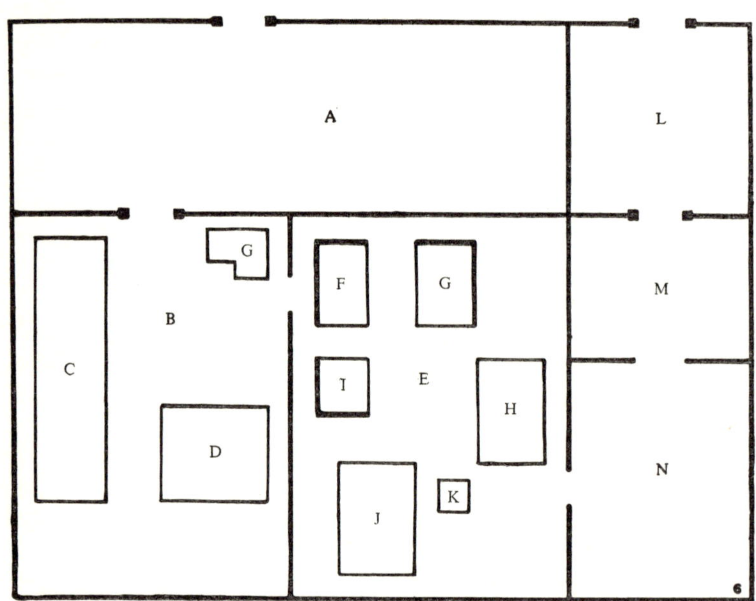


6. Plan of the Puri Pemetjutan, Denpasar. A, Forecourt. B, Second court. C, *Balé lantang*, a pavilion for musical practice. D. *Balairung*, an audience pavilion. E, Inner court. F, *Balé aling aling*. G, Sleeping pavilion for men. H, Sleeping pavilion for women. I, *Balé murdah*, a pavilion for last rites. J, *Balé sari*, a pavilion for religious ceremonies. K, Shrine to the spirit of the palace. L, First temple area. M, Second temple area. N, Sanctuary for the family shrines.

A gate leads to the inner courtyard (E). A small building used for receiving the family guests (F) is now used as an artist's studio. It is called the *balé aling aling*, because it takes the place of the normal *aling aling* wall. The west building (G) is a sleeping pavilion for men. The north building (H), completely walled in, is a sleeping pavilion for women. The south building (I) is known as a *balé murdah* and is the pavilion used for the last rites of the dead before cremation. The east building (J), known as a *balé sari*, is reserved for religious ceremonies such as weddings, tooth filing and so on. The *sanggah pengidjeng* (K) is a small shrine dedicated to the spirit guardians of the Puri.

There are three areas devoted to purely religious purposes. The first area (L) entered from Djalan Thamrin, is the original family temple area, now unoccupied and used for religious dances and ceremonies. A gate leads to the second area (M) which is used for the preparation of temple offerings. The third area (N) is the present family temple containing the family shrines. In this area the shrines are richly decorated and there is a particularly fine example of an elaborate *padmasana* with the base carved in the turtle and snake motif.

KULKUL TOWERS

There are two *kulkul* towers in Denpasar worth close examination. The first of these is on the corner diagonally opposite to the Puri Pemetjutan (see Fig. 5, station 5). This tower is a carved stone one similar to the tower at the museum. It has four tiers with eight statuettes of *raksasas* on each of the first three tiers. The topmost tier is distinguished by having blue Chinese porcelain plates let into the surface as decoration.

The second *kulkul* tower is at Kesiman and is located on Djalan Gianjar opposite the end of Djalan Abiankapas (see Fig. 5, station 8). This is one of the most remarkable *kulkul* towers to be seen in Bali. It is constructed almost exclusively of brick, and nearly all decoration has been carved in the brick itself, which gives the whole structure a strong, warm and rugged feeling. The tower is built essentially in four tiers, each one successively smaller than the one below it.

The first two tiers are similar, having the monstrous face of a *karang tjewiri* in the centre of each side, with figures representing Rawana riding Wilmana on each corner of the first tier, and with mythical figures, half female half bird, on the corners of the second tier. The third tier is decorated with a modified *karang tjewiri* on each side with a stylised Garuda, *karang tjuring*, on each corner. The fourth tier is decorated with a series of small modified demon faces surmounted by a single female face on each side. All four tiers are decorated with white Chinese porcelain plates let into the brickwork. The visitor should make a point of examining this *kulkul* tower in detail.

THE MARKET

The Denpasar market (Plate 24) is entered either from Djalan Gadja Mada (Plate 25), the main street of Denpasar, or from Djalan Sulawesi. Entering from Djalan Gadja Mada the first section traversed is that where hardwares and textiles are sold. This is followed by a section at a lower level which is stocked with a great variety of mats, baskets and bamboo wares and which leads to the food market. Of particular interest is the large section devoted to the sale of spices, nuts and flavourings of all kinds, where the number and variety of spices displayed exceeds that to be seen anywhere else. The balance of the market is given over to the selling of meats, fruit, vegetables and tobacco. The market is always thronged with women in brightly coloured costumes. The activity spills over into Djalan Sulawesi where selling continues, girls search one another's hair for lice, and sticks of *saté* are grilled on little charcoal fires. The market is always full of colour and activity and is well worth a visit.

# 13

# *Mengwi and Sangeh*

The road from Denpasar to Mengwi is a part of the main highway connecting the capital with Singaradja in the north while Sangeh is on a road parallel and to the east of it. The road passes through a succession of rice terraces and villages. Five miles from Denpasar one of the main irrigation channels is passed at Lukluk. The cascading water always provides an attractive scene. A short distance further on there are nurseries for native trees and a small factory processing copra to extract coconut oil for local use. Seven miles from Denpasar the village of Kapal is reached. The village temple, situated on the main road frontage is well worth inspection.

TEMPLE AT KAPAL

The *pura desa* at Kapal is a temple well worth a visit. It has several features of great interest. The outer court is entered through a 'split' gate, a *tjandi bentar* of stone, tall, elegantly carved and guarded by two *raksasas*. To its right is a carved stone *kulkul* tower. The inner shrine is served by a very tall *padu raksa* of brick surmounted by the face of a monster, or *karang tjewiri*, with three carved tiers above it. The doors are elegantly carved, with seven overlintels. A second *padu raksa* of much simpler design is located to the left of it. These are normally kept closed and the inner shrine is approached by a small gate to the right. The rear of the main *padu raksa* is also carved with much elaborate detail (Plate 20). An unusual feature is a number of female figures in various poses.

The wall to the side of the main gate has three carved stone panels incorporated in it, the theme of the carvings being the fable of the monkey and the tortoise. There is a magnificent example of a *gedong pesimpangan* in the inner shrine area. This building stands on a high platform approached by a flight of stone steps carved with *naga* hand-rails. The walls of the shrine are of brick with carved stone inserts. There are two highly-carved gilded doors. The whole is surmounted by a thick thatch of black *idjuk*, and is protected by a series of guardians on the platform.

Just past the village of Kapal the road to Gilimanuk branches to the left and two miles further on is the village of Mengwi. The Pura Pelet here is worth inspection.

THE PURA PELET

The Pura Pelet at Bandjar Pupuan Mengwi has very attractive precincts. The carved stone *tjandi bentar* of the outer entrance is approached via a stone 'bridge' over the moat, which sweeps across the front and down the side of the temple area. The moat is faced with stone and the surface of the water is thickly covered with water lilies. In the right hand front corner of the temple compound is an interesting and attractive *kulkul* tower in brick with carved stone inserts. The base is decorated in each corner with an elephant head motif, the second and third tiers with human figure motifs. Several inset panels are carved with a variety of human figure studies. There are twin 'bells' and the wide roof is thatched with *idjuk*, with the ridges protected by a line of ceramic tiles. The inner gate is of simple design and is similarly thatched and tiled.

At Mengwi, the road proceeding on to Sangeh turns to the right off the Singaradja road and almost immediately it passes the front of the 'Water Temple' of Taman Ajun, built originally by the former King of Mengwi, but now the property of the people of the area. Approached from this direction at a slight elevation, the temple is seen across the water of a wide moat formed by an artificial lake. This moat extends across the front of the temple compound and backwards along the side of the temple and well to the rear of it. The first impression is of a grassed and verdant temple area of considerable extent which appears as an island 'floating' in the water of the moat.

THE TEMPLE OF TAMAN AJUN

The 'Water Temple' of Taman Ajun is probably the most beautiful of all temple precincts in Bali. This is not only because of its lakeside setting, but also by virtue of the sweeping grassed approach, the attractive buildings and gates associated with it, and the exquisite series of *merus* in the very attractive inner shrine area.

The front entrance is a very large *tjandi bentar* approached by a roadway across the moat. This leads to a very large well-grassed area forming the outer courtyard. To the right of the front entrance is one of the largest cockfighting and drama arenas in Bali, a square *wantilan* with a sunken central arena and a high thatched roof in two levels, ventilated between them. It is separated from the main forecourt by a unique wall with a base of brick surmounted by carved stonework decorated with a leaf and flower design. A *tjandi bentar* gives access to the *wantilan* through the wall. To the left of the main gate is an ornate carved stone 'fountain' incorporating turtle and snake motifs which stands in a square, stone-faced, water lily pool. This is a most attractive feature.

Approaching the gateway to the second compound an isolated shrine area is passed on the right. Situated on an elevated stone platform located on a rise, it is approached by a long flight of stone steps and entered through an old thatched *balé*. The platform contains several enclosed shrines with thatched roofs and two interesting carved stone 'altars'. A *tjandi bentar* leads down to the huge *wantilan*.

Steps lead up through a *padu raksa* with a high, pointed, carved top section, to the second compound, which is at a higher elevation. Immediately inside this gate is an isolated masonry shrine with a roof of *idjuk* thatch. The second compound is also completely grassed. A further flight of stone steps leads upward through a second *padu raksa*. The main gateway is closed by carved wooden doors, but small doorways each side of it lead through to the magnificent inner shrine area at a still higher level. This inner area is surrounded by a stone wall, and inside the stone wall is a stone-faced moat extending right round the shrine area with the exception of the entrance. The moat is a tranquil expanse of translucent green water (Plate 18) in which water lily leaves punctuate the reflections of the blue sky and the adjacent *merus* and shrines.

Along the western side of the inner sanctuary, along the edge of the moat is a series of simple open *balés* for the preparation of offerings and one magnificently carved brick and stone shrine with a thatched roof of *idjuk*. Note particularly the representation of Garuda attacking Naga carved on each corner of the base. Along the northern and eastern borders there are ten *merus*. These are of exquisite proportion, tall and thin, with roofs thatched with black *idjuk* fibre (Plate 19). The bases are open, four-posted timber *balés* mounted on carved stone pedestals decorated with guardians and other mythical figures. There are three *merus* with eleven tiers, three with nine tiers, one with seven, one with five and two with three tiers.

On the eastern edge, between the *merus*, is an attractive *gedong pesimpangan*. The design is unusual (Plate 11) in that the front platform is approached by a plain, undecorated set of stone steps, does not extend out from the building the full width of the *alang alang* thatched roof, and in consequence the four wooden 'verandah' posts extend to the ground in front of it and rest on simple brick pediments. The enclosing walls are of brick. The central door in front is highly carved, flanked by two guardians, and has a monstrous face carved over it in the form of a *karang tjewiri* bearing the deer's antlers of Madjapahit. On each side of the door there is a carved stone pierced panel let into the wall in the form of a window.

There are several small but highly decorated shrines carved in brick and stone and on the north side a circular well. Finally there is an elegant stone *padmasana* in the centre of the area (Plate 17), its back towards Gunung Agung, with a three compartment seat to accommodate the trinity of gods.

Continuing past the front of the Taman Ajun temple the road leads to Sangeh. The track is rough and progress necessarily slow, but it traverses a number of quiet and attractive villages with dried mud walls thatched with rice straw and with covered gates similarly thatched. The village of Gutingan (Plate 8) is a good example. Five miles from Mengwi is the sacred wood of Sangeh.

SANGEH—THE SACRED MONKEY FOREST

The sacred forest is an area of some thirty acres of *pala* trees. The timber of the *pala* tree is not of great value, but the trees themselves, in a closely-spaced stand such as the one at Sangeh, grow tall and straight, reaching a height of some 150 feet or more. In consequence the atmosphere of the forest is dark and gloomy and it is extremely damp and overgrown with moss and lichen. The forest is a temple area occupied by large numbers of monkeys which are protected as sacred. They are accustomed to the presence of visitors and flock around them when called by the small boys inevitably present at the entrance. These boys sell peanuts which the visitors feed to the monkeys—that is if the monkeys do not snatch them away before the visitors have a chance to begin feeding them.

The forest is entered through a typical split gate, from which a path leads along the southern edge of the forest. The visitor walks along this path accompanied by hordes of monkeys and youthful mendicants, finally arriving at the main approach to the Monkey Temple. The temple itself is located in the centre of the wood. A wide straight roadway cuts a swathe through the trees and leads straight to the temple gate. There is but one temple compound entered through a *tjandi bentar* at the top of a short flight of stone steps. Immediately behind the entrance gate is a large carved statue of Garuda attacking Naga. This is heavily coated with moss and is a favourite playground for the monkeys. The sanctuary contains a number of simple wooden *balés* thatched with *idjuk*. There is one attractive *idjuk*-thatched *meru* of nine tiers on a turtle and snake stone base embellished with white porcelain plates. Under the lowest tier of thatch is an enclosure of carved and gilt wood with monkey motifs.

The atmosphere in the forest is one of isolation and cold loneliness. One senses the inevitable destructive processes of nature under conditions which are cold and damp even on a hot summery day. It is quite a relief to leave the sacred temple area to the monkeys, whose property it is, and to return again to warmth and sunshine.

# 14

## *Denpasar to Mas and Ubud*

The main road to the east from Denpasar commences with Djalan Gianjar. The carved brick *kulkul* tower opposite the end of Djalan Abiankapas has already been discussed in Chapter 12. Immediately following it several temple precincts attached to the village of Kesiman are passed. They are worth inspection by the visitor who has sufficient time.

The first river passed is the River Ajung. Not a large river, but nevertheless the longest in Bali. Here by the bridge the sand gatherers are always active, whilst just over the bridge on the right is the modern weaving mill of Balitex. Not far beyond it, on the left, is the complementary yarn-spinning mill of Patal Tohpati. At the village of Tegeha, the road turns sharply to the left and traverses a patch of open rice fields. The presence of a carved stone guardian at the corner protects the traveller from harm. In the morning men and women can often be seen here carrying home the harvested rice in sheaves on their shoulders and on their heads. Women carrying heavy loads of clay pottery piled high in apparent confusion on their heads can also be seen going to nearby markets. The rice fields give way again to coconut palms and verdant growth as the village of Batubulan is reached.

### THE TEMPLE OF BATUBULAN

The temple of Batubulan is the background against which one of the best performances of the Barong Play to be seen in Bali is given. The forecourt is the stage, the *tjandi bentar* of the sanctuary serves as the point of entry and exit for the players. The pavilions in the sanctuary become the actors' dressing rooms. Here, before the play begins, the men of the village can be seen applying make-up and decorating their faces with fierce, upturned and pointed moustaches. Women can be seen creating the crowns of flowers which become the attractive and exquisite head dresses of the *legong* dancers, who at that stage, without their magnificent costumes, are almost unrecognisable as such. To house the spectators there is a bamboo and thatch structure to provide shade from the sun, and a similar but smaller structure protects the *gamelan* orchestra.

The temple itself is worth inspection apart from its interest as the scene of regular Barong performances. In particular the beautiful *gedong pesimpangan* should be noted (Plate 14). It is a completely enclosed brick and stone building with a short flight of stone steps leading directly to the carved wooden doorway. On each side a guardian gives protection. There is a four tier overlintel surmounted by the monstrous face of a *karang tjewiri,* and above this a carved stone gable end completes the building. Shrubs and flowers growing in the sanctuary create a pleasant and restful atmosphere.

Not far beyond Batubulan a road junction marks the village of Tegaltamu. The road to the right leads on to Tjeluk, Mas and Ubud. The road straight ahead leads immediately into the village of Singapadu. This is another centre where an excellent Barong Dance is staged every week in front of the village temple.

THE VILLAGE TEMPLE OF SINGAPADU

Here again the needs of the spectators are met by the erection of a viewing pavilion and an orchestra stand in the temple forecourt. The arena is immediately in front of the main gate of the temple, a large *tjandi bentar* protected by a pair of guardians, by which the performers enter and leave the arena. In front of the gate is a wide platform with steps leading down to the main dancing area. It is down these steps that the dancers proceed in slow progression as their introduction to the audience. As in the case of Batubulan, the temple precincts themselves are worthy of close inspection. Just inside the main gate is a *gedong pesimpangan* of entirely different character. The door is located under the gable end of the thatched roof, which overhangs the end of the brick building it protects. Two brick pillars, one on either side of the doorway, support the overhanging roof.

The pillars are decorated with a *naga* motif in carved stone. An elaborate carved *karang tjewiri* surmounts the door, which is covered by a simple woven bamboo screen, and carved figures of priests holding their bells, flank the doorway on either side.

The black *idjuk*-thatched shrines in brick and stone are attractively designed, again with overhanging roofs supported in front by twin wooden pillars. To the left of the main entrance, on the corner of the walled sanctuary, is a twin *kulkul* tower thatched with *idjuk*. Though not very large, this masonry tower is elaborately carved. The lowest tier shows elephant-head motifs, the second tier is decorated with *karang tjuring* designs. The third tier is similar and the fourth tier is decorated with carvings of *singhasaris*, or winged lions.

When dance performances are being held the street is thronged with mendicants selling wood and ivory carvings, *kris, lontar* books and other novelties, and in particular, *batik* cloth. The latter is sold by girls who carry their stock-in-trade piled up high on their heads. *Batik* can be bought here at very reasonable prices.

ROCK CARVING AT TEGALTAMU

Tegaltamu, at the road junction, is one of the main centres of stone carving in Bali. Here there are several 'shops' where men and boys, some extraordinarily young, sit by the roadside (Plate 34) in the shade of overhanging roofs and trees, carving elaborate figures from the soft, volcanic siltstone gathered not far away in the deeply-dissected bed of the River Petanu. The carver sits, either on a stool or cross-legged on the ground, and carves the detailed decoration on roughly-shaped blocks of stone, using simple steel chisels of different shapes. So soft is the freshly-cut rock that it is easier to carve than wood. No mallet is normally necessary, the chisels being manipulated by hand. After carving, the rock gradually hardens as it dries out, but it never becomes really resistant to weathering influences. It has the attraction, however, that in a warm, humid atmosphere such as prevails in Bali, it very quickly acquires a mossy patina which gives an appearance of considerable age. A wide variety of carved

figures may be inspected as displayed in the shops at Tegaltamu. Prices are very reasonable, but the problems of pack-
ing and transport abroad, at the present time, are considerable.

## TJELUK AND ITS SILVERWARE

Shortly after leaving Tegaltamu a series of shops by the
roadside at Tjeluk display silver jewellery for sale. In one
of these, 'Sura', the actual manufacture of silver jewellery
and ornaments can be watched. The basic form of the product, such as a ring or brooch, is made by silver-soldering
a brass framework. On this is built up the silver ornamenta-
tion, by coating the object with adhesive and placing tiny
globules of silver on it. The silver is then melted with a
blowpipe to form a coating on the product being made, the
adhesive also acting as a flux. The finished jewellery is a
finely executed product of delicate and appealing design. It
is made in a wide range of styles and types.

## TJEMENGGON

After passing Tjeluk the road leads to the suspension
bridge over the River Oos (pronounced Owos). Just before
reaching the river, the main entrance gate of the temple of
Tjemenggon should be noted. It is unusual because it is
constructed as a triple gate, the main central gateway being
flanked by two smaller gateways, each in the form of a separate structure, connected by the sanctuary wall. All three
gates are in *padu raksa* form. It is unusual also, because the
stonework on the gates is substantially undecorated, being
simply but carefully carved to the stylised broad shapes of
the decorative elements with no embellishment except for
a simple face over each doorway and simple *naga* and
guardian motifs in front.

The River Oos is one of considerable size and at most
times of the day, but more particularly in the early morning
and in the evening, people can be seen bathing in the cool
waters, the men to the north of the bridge, the women to the
south of it. After crossing the bridge the road again turns to
the left and enters the village of Sukowati.

THE SUKOWATI MARKET

Sukowati is a long village and is distinguished by an active and colourful local market. The market is held, for the main part, in a rather wide cross street in the middle of the village (Plate 5). Here small stalls shaded by woven palm-leaf panels erected above them, are loaded with the usual produce seen in markets—fruit, vegetables, meats, tobacco, rice, spices of all kinds, woven goods, mats and clothing. The market is thronged with women, both bare breasted and clothed in their colourful *kains* and *kebajas*. This market is of interest to the visitor as an example of an ordinary village market in which the ordinary villagers are seen making their daily purchases, stopping to talk or enjoy a drink or a little food.

A mile further on the road passes over a rise, bends to the left and reveals the art shops of Batuan.

BATUAN—AN ART CENTRE

There are several art shops at Batuan which display a variety of wood carvings and paintings. Here both wood carvers and painters can be seen at work in open pavilions at the roadside. Wood carving is done by the carvers squatting on the floor. The piece being carved is rested on a block of wood for support and held firm by one of the carver's feet. A series of some thirty fine steel chisels is used, always in conjunction with a wooden mallet, the strokes of which are extremely light and delicate. The carving develops under the carver's hand without reference to a model. Various carvers become expert in certain designs. Most are finished by using successively finer glass papers and finally polished with wax, but some carvings are painted in gay colours. Painting is likewise done without reference to a model. The painter squats cross-legged on the floor of his pavilion in

PLATE 49. The Kerta Gosa, the old courthouse at Klungkung. The underside of the roof is decorated with magnificent murals depicting the fate of sinners in hell. The pillars supported on carved animals are of particular interest.

PLATE 50. The main concourse in the old Bali Aga village of Tenganan. Note the unusual appearance of the family compounds due to the building of the formal pavilion immediately behind the front wall.

front of his canvas (Plate 33). He first makes a drawing in pencil and shades it with black. Casein tempera paints are used. These are mixed with water as the vehicle. The black and white shaded drawing is finally overpainted with semi-transparent washes of colour to produce the typical Balinese style of painting.

Associated with one of the art shops (Dwarawadi) is a fine cloth weaving section. Colourful designs are woven by young girls sitting at the simple typical Balinese looms located in an open pavilion (Plate 22). The cloths woven are of narrow width and short length. They are normally sashes, binders and scarves, and many are made in imported artificial silk materials. Methods of pattern development are always interesting to watch.

After passing Batuan the road turns to the right and continues for two miles through the villages of Mawan and Sakah. These villages always seem quiet and peaceful, activity if present being hidden behind the long succession of thatched, dried-mud walls regularly broken by the thatched entry gates leading to individual family compounds. Beyond Sakah the road divides once more, that to the right being the main road to Gianjar and the east, that straight on leading to Mas.

MAS—CENTRE OF WOOD CARVING

After leaving the Gianjar road the way leads through a gently rising succession of rice terraces set in open country. Here harvesting may often be seen, and on clear days the sight of the symmetrical, barren cone of Gunung Agung rising pale purple in the distance provides an inspiring background to the scene. As the rice *sawahs* give way again to luxuriant tropical vegetation, the village of Mas begins. Here a number of exhibition centres displaying both paint-

---

PLATE 51. The 'Mother Temple' at Besakih. The *meru* on the right is the original shrine. The high rising front of the main court draws the eye naturally past the split gate to the peak of 10,308 ft. Mt. Agung behind the temple.

PLATE 52. The 'Kings' *merus*' at Besakih. These *merus* are unique in that they are constructed entirely of brick and mortar. Here repose the souls of the former Radjas of Bali.

I

ings and wood carvings, are located. The latter predominate, because Mas is the acknowledged centre of the wood carver's art. It is the home of a very senior carver, Ida Bagus Njana, well-respected and with a widely-acknowledged reputation. His family carry on the business today under the name of Ida Bagus Tilem, and in the family compound attached to the display pavilion, Ida Bagus Njana can nearly always be seen carving figures in unusual woods in an unusual style (Plate 36) which will undoubtedly have a profound effect on the future trend of Balinese carving. His recent and advanced work is displayed in the exhibition of Ida Bagus Tilem in the centre of Mas. Almost opposite is another display of excellent wood carving in the establishment of Adil. Both these establishments are attached to family compounds of wealth. The visitor should take the opportunity of inspecting not only the wood carvers actually working in these compounds, but the compounds themselves. The beauty and richness of the internal decoration of these compounds is quite remarkable. In particular one should not miss seeing the simple but delicate tracery of the *balé sari* used for formal religious occasions, in the Tilem compound, and the unusual carved-stone, gilt and *idjuk*-covered shrines and the magnificent *umah metén* in the Adil compound (Plates 12, 23).

At the Barwa studios, located amongst the *sawahs* just prior to entering the village of Mas itself, a selection of Balinese paintings is always on view, and is distinguished by the consistently good quality of the exhibits.

Alongside the Adil establishment an open grassed area leads past the inevitable *waringin* tree to the temple of Mas, the Pura Tamansari. Here the villagers hold many lavish festivals (Plate 10), including at times, performances of the *wayang wong*. Here the back streets and lanes of the village converge and the visitor obtains a very different picture of the quiet and restful atmosphere of the ordinary Balinese village.

The road beyond Mas ends in a T-junction at Teges. This is the main village centre where the *wantilan* is located. Cockfights and drama are held here. Small shops on the roadside provide food and drink. To the right the road leads to Bedulu, to the left it leads to Peliatan and Ubud. The houses and studios of many painters are now to be seen by the roadside, and shortly after leaving Teges there is a small sanctuary whose shrines are built on a square island round which a moat has been formed.

After turning to the right, the road enters the village of Peliatan. Here in the centre of the village is a large open area with the usual large *waringin* tree growing in it. And next to the open ground is the village temple, the *pura desa* of Peliatan. The temple is notable for its extensive forecourt, its large *padu raksa* and the circular arena in front of it. Here in the velvet blackness of the tropical night, regular performances of the Ketjak Dance are given. It is a remarkable sight to see the many villagers dressed in their short black and white checked sarongs with red and white blossoms over their ears and bare chests, making their cheerful way to the temple to present the performance. Peliatan merges imperceptibly into Ubud, the recognised centre of art and literature in Bali.

UBUD

In the centre of Ubud amongst the giant *waringin* trees is a succession of important buildings. They are adjacent to the large covered market place. First amongst these is the *puri* of the Tjokorde Agung, the former Prince of Ubud. The *puri* is, like the Puri Pemetjutan in Denpasar, a succession of walled courtyards, each one leading to another through a series of *padu raksas*. The outer court is entered from the market square through a covered gateway of unusual style in that the opening is wide and has a semicircular brick arch at the top. In the outer courtyard there is a display of woven materials, a sleeping *balé*, and old pavilions now used for parking motor vehicles. A large and ornate, elevated *padu raksa* leads to the first of the inner courts, but the laborious ascent and descent on the other side, can be avoided by using a small door at ground level on the side. The inner courts are attractively planted with shrubs and flowers. The gates leading from one to another are carved and decorated *padu raksas* complete with *aling aling* walls. Each courtyard contains an enclosed *balé* for sleeping, with communal meeting and eating facilities in the central court. The *puri* is operated as a tourist hotel nowadays, the Tjokorde's own quarters being at the rear. Adjoining the *puri* is the Pura Taman Sari, the family temple of the Royal Princes of Ubud, entered from a platform over a high sill approached by a steep flight of steps. The inner sanctuary is notable for the large number of porcelain plates incorporated in the bases of the shrines.

Next to the market, facing the main roadway is the façade of the Pura Langon. This is an old temple sanctuary not normally available to the public. The front wall contains a central *padu raksa* with a smaller one at either extremity. The notable feature is the large reflecting pool (Plate 21) which covers the full width of the front of the temple. Here the reflection of the sky and the temple frontage amongst the water lilies is a delight to see. The Pura Langon is the seat of the spirits or souls of the Royal Family of Ubud after the dead have been cremated.

A deeply dissected, narrow river bed runs alongside the road next to the Pura Langon. It is crossed by a bridge which leads upwards through pleasant gardens and lawns to a long thatched building. This is the Art Museum of Ubud. It possesses an excellent, if limited, collection of paintings and wood carvings, and is representative of the best work of the leading artists who have worked in Bali. As a background for comparison with the works offered for sale in the studios and exhibition buildings which abound in this area in particular, a visit to the Art Museum is rewarding, and it is particularly informative to those genuinely interested in the historic development of Balinese art.

Opposite to the entrance to the Art Museum there are several buildings exhibiting paintings, and in the side streets of the village many painters live and practise their art. The home of Han Snel, a Dutch painter who has lived in Bali for some twenty years, includes buildings and landscaping of impeccable taste.

# 15

# *Bedulu, Pedjeng and Tampaksiring*

Bedulu is reached either from the Mas-Ubud road by turning right at Teges, or by taking the main Gianjar road from Sakah and turning north at Blahbatu, proceeding via Buruan and Kutri. The visitor should go by both these routes since both include places of great interest. The former leads across a series of terraced rice fields which are particularly fascinating where they descend the steep-walled valley of the River Petanu and ascend it again to continue on the other side. The western outskirts of Bedulu are reached at the 'Elephant Cave', or Goa Gadja. The latter route crosses many more rice terraces which become spectacular and unbelievably beautiful where the road also crosses the River Petanu. Turning the corner at Blahbatu there is an old *puri* and on any day an active street market is in full swing. North towards Bedulu is the village of Kutri, where at the sanctuary of Bukit Darma the famous statue of Mahendradatta rests. The road on to Bedulu passes northward through the village on its way to Pedjeng, Tampaksiring and finally up the western flank of Gunung Agung, the Peak of Bali, to the lip of the caldera-crater of Mt. Batur at Penelokan. The following notes refer to the main items of interest to be seen in this area, which contains most of the oldest antiquities still remaining in Bali.

THE 'ELEPHANT CAVE' AT BEDULU

The River Petanu, like the River Pakrisan, is considered a holy river by the Balinese. Just west of the village of Bedulu it has cut a deep ravine. Here in the side of the valley on a level platform is a sunken bath (Plate 42) of rectangular shape. Steps lead down into it on the western side, while water issues from water pots held by six female, human figures carved in the stone wall forming the eastern side. Above the terrace to the north, is a vertical rock face in which there is a small cave. The cave itself is T-shaped and contains a figure of Ganesa flanked on each side by *linggas* devoted to the trinity of gods. It is not the inside of the cave however, which is remarkable, but the outside. Here the cliff face has been carved to represent the head of a giant monster (Plate 41) in typical guise, with bulging eyes, who splits the rock open at the cave entrance with his hands. Surrounding this figure are representations of people and animals in a formalised, symbolic, forest landscape.

This cave is known as the Goa Gadja, or 'Elephant Cave'. The name is thought by some to have been derived from the figure of Ganesa contained in it and by others to have been derived from the former name of the River Petanu, Air Gadjah, or 'elephant river'. The Balinese ascribe the carving of the cave to the mythical giant Kbo Iwa. Historically it dates from the eighth century and artistically it belongs to the classical period when Balinese art was under Hindu-Javanese influence. A small monastery is established adjacent to it, and above it on the roadside a series of colourful and attractive stalls (Plate 3) sell an extraordinary variety of excellent woven baskets made in the nearby village of Bona from dried leaves of the *lontar* palm.

### KUTRI

Kutri is a village not far to the southeast of Bedulu on the road from Blahbatu. Here there is a most attractive temple set well back from the road at the far end of an open space with a background of deep green tropical foliage covering a steep hill immediately behind it which rises perhaps a hundred feet above it. This is the sanctuary of Bukit Darma. A flight of stone steps set in the hillside leads to the top, where in a *balé* set on a small platform surrounded by guardians there is preserved a fine carved stele representing Mahendradatta, Erlangga's mother, in the form of Giri Putri, wife of Siwa. This statue is a relic of the classical period in Balinese art and is still well-preserved although damaged and broken on the face and legs. The sanctuary is said to be the burial place of Mahendradatta, but no real evidence has been forthcoming. As an important archaeological relic and work of art, it is well worth while inspecting.

PEDJENG

The village of Pedjeng was formerly a part of Bedulu, seat of the early King of Bedulu. There are some forty temples in Pedjeng, but of these only three are of importance. Pura Panataram Sasih is one of the six holy national temples, or Sadkahyangan. It was at one time the royal temple of Bedulu, but most of the original structure was destroyed by an earthquake in 1937. Only two of the original shrines remain today, the remainder having been newly erected during reconstruction in 1967. The original shrines are in brick and carved stone, and in one of these an ancient bronze drum known as the 'Moon Face' reposes. The drum, which is supported just beneath the roof of the structure, is a very large one. The striking end is some five feet in diameter, the body of the drum being some seven feet long with four supporting rings cast integral with it. The general form suggests a Chinese origin, but the decorative motifs cast on the surface make it clear that the drum is Javanese in character, although its exact history is unknown.

Balinese legend has it that there were once two moons. These two moons kept the world continuously illuminated, so that night and day were unknown. A thief, finding it difficult to operate without cover of darkness, ascended to the sky and by urinating on one of the moons caused it to fall to earth. It came to rest in Pedjeng in the form of a bronze drum, slightly broken as a consequence of its fall, and has been safely preserved there ever since, so that night now inevitably follows every day.

The drum certainly dates from the ninth century, and is a relic of the classical period of Balinese art which is of great interest.

Nearby is the equally ancient Pura Pusering Djagat. The temple is reached by a side lane and stands on a high platform overlooking a descending cascade of rice terraces. A grassy sward leads to a massive outer gateway of recent construction, guarded by symbolic elephants. An inner courtyard leads through two split gates to the sanctuary. Here are several ancient stone shrines with carved panels, containing numerous statues and relics of classical times. In one of these is a stone urn for holy water which has been carved with an intricate design of mythical figures. In another place a flat circular stone covers a well which is said to be one end of a tunnel reaching to the island of Nusa Penida. The stone is considered so holy, that no one dares to move it to see what lies beneath!

Almost next to this temple are a few remains constituting all that is left of the Pura Kebo Edan. Here are several statues in quite a good state of preservation which are undoubtedly classical in origin. There are two buffaloes at rest with their heads turned back and supported by their bodies in characteristic fashion. Adjacent to these are two figures with a number of skulls around the crowns of the heads. There is also the remains of an old altar stone carved with many human skulls, and a figure said to represent a mad son of the King of Bedulu. The latter is shown standing on a human body, with a snake entwined with each leg. It is interesting to note that the words '*kebo edan*' mean 'buffalo mad'.

The relics in these three temples at Pedjeng are very good examples of the classical style belonging to the Javanese-Hindu period. They date from the ninth century, and are well worth inspection by all those interested in antiquities.

GUNUNG KAWI—THE KING'S TOMBS

North of Pedjeng and approaching Tampaksiring, a short turn-off to the east reaches the head of a long series of descending stone steps which lead down through a series of spectacular and steep rice terraces into the wide and deep valley of the River Pakrisan. From the upper section of the steps the view across the steep slope of the valley to the cliffs on the opposite side is unexpected and magnificent. Here the water flows from terrace to terrace in a never-ending stream, gradually making its way to the lowest levels and back into the river itself for re-use lower down the valley. In no place can one get a more satisfying impression of the wonderful system of irrigation which the Balinese have developed over so many centuries by continuous practical application. Across the valley, carved in the cliffs of soft volcanic ash, are five mausoleums (Plate 43). These take the form of arched recesses in the rock face, carved in the conical ascending form of ancient burial towers. The largest is said to be the resting place of the ashes of King Anak Wungsu, youngest brother of Erlangga, who was proclaimed King of Bali after Erlangga's death. He reigned over Bali for twenty-eight years from 1049 to 1077 A.D. The other mausoleums are those of his children, while on the opposite side are four further niches said to be the graves of his wives. Next to the King's mausoleum there is a monastery with rectangular recesses carved out of the face of the cliffs. The whole complex of tombs and cells, called the Gunung Kawi, and known alternatively as the King's Tombs, belongs to the eleventh century and shows the Hindu-Javanese classical influence. At that time, cremation had not become customary in Bali, and it is thought that the cells cut in the face of the cliff were used for disposing of the dead by exposure to the elements and wild animals. The tombs were discovered only as recently as 1920, but were actually known to the Balinese long before this. Their belief was that they had been carved by the mythical hands of the giant Kbo Iwa.

TIRTA EMPUL—THE HOLY SPRING

A little farther up the holy Pakrisan River, a road descending to the floor of the valley leads to the holy springs and temple of Tirta Empul. Here in a rectangular stone basin filled with crystal-clear water, the springs can be seen issuing continuously from the sandy bed. Veneration of this place is so deep that the water from these springs is accepted as holy water for religious rites, although when blessed by a priest its holiness is considerably enhanced.

Below the springs the water issues from the mouths of water pots carved in a long stone wall, and here both men and women bathe in the refreshing and holy water separated only by a low wall of stone. These public baths, entered as is a temple, through a large *tjandi bentar*, are very popular and well-patronised.

On a terrace above the baths, alongside the holy spring itself, is the temple of Tirta Empul. This is one of the six most holy national temples. The temple has recently undergone renovation and reconstruction, and the shrines in its sanctuary (Plate 44) are most attractively decorated. Completely enclosed, with carved wooden doors, they are gilded and painted in vivid colours to which the black *idjuk* roofs provide a magnificent contrast.

Overlooking the valley and the whole temple area is an impressive but unused guest house, built in the days of Soekarno, a luxury the government cannot afford to maintain today. It is built in two sections on two prominences and these are connected by a footbridge carried on a high arched support. There are many permanent stalls stocked with carvings, woven goods, baskets and similar items, located along the approach road and adjacent to the temple area. On the day of Kuninggan the temple's birthday is celebrated by a festival noted for its size and magnificence, and people come from considerable distances to join in the festivities on this occasion.

# 16

# Gianjar, Bangli and Lake Batur

Between Bedulu and Gianjar the road crosses the sacred River Pakrisan. Here again the rice terraces are a delight to behold, but they soon give way to a more mundane landscape as the outskirts of Gianjar are reached. Gianjar, home of a former Radja, is now an administrative and commercial town of very modest size and no distinction. Continuing east the road crosses the deep terraced gorge of the River Sangsang and shortly afterwards the road to Bangli and the north turns off the eastern highway to the left. Almost immediately it begins to climb steeply through a succession of ascending rice terraces. On a bend of the road overlooking Gianjar is an attractive and noteworthy temple. This is the *pura dalem*, the cemetery temple, of Sidan.

THE PURA DALEM OF SIDAN

A stone wall sweeps around the wide bend of the road. A highly-carved twin *kulkul* tower with a wide tiled roof is located right on the corner itself and to the left of it the outer compound of the temple is entered through a *tjandi bentar* set in an elaborate temple wall in front of which are several carved stone *raksasas*, or guardians. The inner sanctuary is entered by a most elaborate *padu raksa* gateway having a carved stone fin ascending in a smooth unbroken curve tapering from base to top. The shrines in the inner sanctuary are of course, few in number since this is a cemetery temple, the home of Betari Durga. They are supported on bases profusely adorned with carved human figures. The shrines themselves are enclosed and covered by wide, spreading, tiled roofs. This is an inspiring temple to study in detail. It commands an extensive view over the surrounding rice terraces.

129

THE PURA KEHEN AT BANGLI

Continuing northwards the town of Bangli is reached after five miles. Bangli is a market town and a centre of carving of coconut-shell ornaments. Beyond the town, nestling under the shelter of a steep hillside rising to an elevation of 2,000 feet, is the sacred Temple of Kehen. The temple is composed of three courts. Because it is located on a steep hillside these three courts rise one above the other at successively higher elevations. The outer court is reached from the roadway by a flight of forty steps ascending through a series of garden terraces and lined with five guardians on each side. It is entered through a *padu raksa* stone gate with a central opening as well as two smaller side gates in the same structure. The central gate has attractive carved wooden doors and is framed by an elegant surround cut in the stonework of the structure. Access to the outer court may also be had from the terrace in front of it by either of two smaller 'split' gates located at each end of the front wall. A very large *waringin* tree grows in the outer courtyard and the temple *kulkul* platform is mounted in this tree. A series of fourteen steps leads upwards to the level of the second courtyard. Here are pavilions for the preparation of offerings and a large stone, said to be a holy stone, part of a monastery previously established on the site. Entrance to the second court is by a 'split' gate. A series of twelve further steps leads upwards through still another 'split' gate to the third and last courtyard, the inner sanctuary. Here are the shrines and *merus* dedicated to the gods.

This arrangement of a *padu raksa* entrance to the outer court with *tjandi bentar* 'split' gates giving access to the inner courts, is not unique, but is unusual. There are few exceptions to the customary arrangement of a *tjandi bentar* outer gate followed by a *padu raksa* entrance to the inner courts.

In the sanctuary area the chief point of interest is a magnificent eleven-tiered *meru* dedicated to Siwa, which can be seen immediately the final 'split' gate is approached. It is well worth careful study. The low stone base is reached by six small stone steps in front. The bottom layer is carved in the representation of a turtle whose head, surmounted by the snout of a pig, protrudes from the second step. The accompanying snake motif takes the form of two *nagas* arranged so as to form the balustrades each side of the front steps. The figures of six angels and guardians adorn the front of the platform which supports an elaborately-carved stone enclosure bearing a pair of carved and gilded wooden doors. This building supports the hollow central core of the *meru* which carries the series of eleven diminishing roofs carefully thatched with the black fibre of *idjuk*. The lowest tier of the roof is very wide and gives the effect of a sweeping curved outline to the pagoda-like structure. This is one of the best examples of a *meru* to be seen in Bali.

In the right hand corner, with its back to Gunung Agung, is a stone *padmasana* covered with a wealth of detail, including human figures. Such is the Temple of Kehen, the *pura desa* and *pura panataran* of Bangli, a very holy temple indeed.

The road north from the temple area to Lake Batur is a poor one. It is better to return to Bangli and turn right onto the road which meets another coming from Tampaksiring at the village of Seribatu. This road rises steadily from Bangli passing through a series of villages set in a succession of wide, unirrigated terraces where various fodder crops, tapioca, sweet potato and corn are grown. The atmosphere grows cooler, even on a sunny day. The character of the villages changes in a subtle and almost imperceptible way. There is a gradual change from the low-pitched roofs thatched with *alang alang* to a very much steeper style, where the height of the roof approximates twice the width, and grass thatch gives way to bamboo shingles. No doubt these changes have been found advantageous in the areas of heavier rainfall. The eaves overhang the walls by a large margin. The walls become exclusively of woven bamboo which later gives way to a horizontal timber boarding in the Lake Batur area. A typical village exhibiting the highland characteristics is Sekardadi with its one long, straight village street traversing it at a level well below that of the family compounds, so that the road appears to lie in a cutting. Sekardadi, a very old village, is reached only two miles before the road arrives at the edge of the caldera of Lake Batur at Penelokan at an elevation of 4,500 feet.

LAKE BATUR

On a clear day Mt. Agung is seen to the east as one travels from Bangli to Penelokan, and its cone becomes more pointed and symmetrical in appearance as the journey proceeds. More often than not, however, the bare, lava-encrusted 10,308 foot peak is enshrouded in cloud and mist, even in the dry season. As the road approaches Penelokan the adjacent Mt. Abang, 7,058 feet high, can be seen to the east. At Penelokan the road turns sharply left to the west and runs along the crest which forms the edge of the caldera which contains Lake Batur (Plate 1) and the mountain of the same name.

The sudden change in outlook is breathtaking. The comparatively flat, but ascending landscape has suddenly disappeared, and in its place a veritable abyss appears. The edge of the caldera falls away almost sheer below the road to the north, and forms a huge basin, roughly circular in plan, some seven miles across. The floor of the depression is nearly 1,500 feet below the road. In the eastern section of it is Lake Batur, a magnificent sheet of placid, blue water five miles long and two miles wide with the face of the caldera rising abruptly above it to the summit of Mt. Abang. In the very centre of the caldera is the volcanic cone of Mt. Batur which rises to a height of 5,633 feet and is therefore more than 1,000 feet higher than the village of Penelokan. Mt. Batur last erupted in 1926 when the village of Batur on the western end of the lake was completely destroyed. The mountain still emits a plume of steam and vapour today, more than forty years later. The steam is said to result from the seepage of moisture to the still-hot layers of lava well below the surface. The dark, chocolate-brown lava extends from the top of the cone to the floor of the caldera, broken only by one small conical hill of verdant green projecting through it halfway down the south side.

Since the destruction of the village of Batur in 1926 there has been no re-establishment of villages on the western side of the lake, but there are several ancient villages located on the eastern edge under the shadow of Mt. Abang. These villages, including Trunyan, where many old Bali Aga practices still exist, are accessible only by boat. The whole panorama of the Lake Batur region is laid out in front of the visitor at a vantage point located a short distance west of the village of Penelokan, from which both Mt. Abang and Mt. Agung behind it can be seen at the same time.

## THE VILLAGE OF BATUR

From Penelokan the road is no longer surfaced and it is dry and dusty, especially in the dry season. It follows the edge of the caldera very closely as it wends its way westwards, climbing still higher as it goes. At the village of Batur, established on the edge of the caldera subsequent to the destruction of the former village of Batur in 1926, the road has reached an elevation approximating 5,000 feet. The visitor will note that the mountain people in this area feel the cold and wear the *kamen*, a type of blanket *cum* garment, round their shoulders for warmth. The village itself is no longer a succession of walled family compounds. In the mountain areas of north Bali the houses are to a large extent individual units widely dispersed in the forest country and amongst the plantations. The villages consist of a small congregation of houses assembled informally, and the traditional arrangement with walls and individual contiguous family compounds does not exist. The village of Batur is of this character. Here on the very edge of the caldera is the Temple of Ulun Danu which has been built to replace that destroyed by the lava flows in 1926. Although relatively new and as yet unfinished, the temple is remarkable for the very high and slender carved stone *padu raksa* which constitutes the main entrance to the outer courtyard. It is simply carved in formalised shapes and has a representation of an eleven-tiered *meru* roof above the gateway, each tier being decorated with a pair of human figures. The entrance to the inner shrine is a simple *tjandi bentar*, so that as in the case of the Temple of Kehen at Bangli, the types of entrances are reversed from normal practice. The inner sanctuary contains a very large number of small individual shrines placed so that they overlook the mountain that destroyed their predecessors. The view from the temple area over the caldera and lake is magnificent, and the constant sight of the quietly-smoking mountain as a background to the new temple serves as a grim reminder of the fate that befell the old one. The village is almost continuous with Kintamani, an old market town where in former times the Dutch administration maintained a well-known rest house. Here the market is usually held in the main street since there is normally little traffic.

From Batur and Kintamani the road continues to rise until it reaches its summit where it leaves the edge of the caldera under the shadow of Mt. Panulisan, 5,720 feet above sea level. The country here becomes a little more verdant. There are many fine stands of *Pinus mercusi* and *Macrocarpus*. The road commences to descend the mountains through forests of increasing density and increasing beauty. Travelling is necessarily slow because of the very bad state of repair of the road, but this allows more time for the visitor to enjoy the steep descent by a road flanked with lantanas and ferns passing through dense groves of *Casuarina* and areas ablaze with the brilliant red blossoms of the dominant *dapdap*, or Indian Coral Tree. The steep-roofed, bamboo-shingled, timber-boarded type of house still persists. Villages are unconventional and even hedges are to be seen in them. Coffee plantations become frequent and there are many jackfruit trees and *taro* plants. At Tamblang, a semi-walled village of lime mortar and volcanic pebble construction, the road re-enters an area of rice terraces and coconut palms, and the narrow northern lowlands lie ahead, extending to the blue sea beyond.

# 17

# *Northern Bali and Lake Bratan*

Northern Bali is at once similar and yet different to southern Bali. The area is a lowland sloping gently from the central mountain ranges to the northern seaboard, which is terraced for rice culture and is covered with verdant patches of coconut palms, tropical fruits and bamboos in which the villages are located, and is similar to the southern lowlands in this regard. The area of usable lowlands however is restricted to some fifty square miles in the Singaradja area and to some twenty square miles in the Seririt area. The climate is perceptibly hotter and although the lowlands are situated close to the foothills of the mountains, the country is more arid. The annual rainfall is but half of that falling in the south. These factors tend to combine to endow the north with a very different atmosphere to that of the south, an atmosphere suggestive of an indolent life under hot, dry, parched and dusty conditions.

The main towns of the north—Kubutambahan, Sangsit, Buleleng and Singaradja—seem to lack activity and have an air of hopelessness rather than an air of progress and happy communal living. There is little doubt that this has been engendered by the gradual decline in shipping into the 'port' of Buleleng until it consists only of a few trading boats travelling under sail from nearby islands, and by the removal of governmental administration to Denpasar.

In the north, the temples, which in the south constitute the backbone of the country and the mainstay of the people, seem to be little used. In the main, although originally of great beauty and character, the temples appear to be unused, neglected and deteriorating. Nevertheless they are of considerable interest because of the 'rococo' character of their decoration and the different arrangement of their components. It will be remembered that to the Balinese, 'north' is towards the mountains, 'south' is towards the sea. In southern Bali, the Balinese 'north' and 'south' and true north and south are more or less identical. In northern Bali however, the Balinese 'north' becomes true south and the Balinese 'south' becomes true north. But to the Balinese 'east' is always true east, for that is where the sun rises, and 'west' is always true west, for that is where the sun sets. These curious concepts must be borne in mind when looking at temples in northern Bali, where the visitor will note that the sanctuary areas are on the southeastern aspect and the entrances on the northern or western aspect.

### KUBUTAMBAHAN

The road from the Lake Batur area descends through heavily forested country into the lowlands at Tamblang and three miles later reaches the coast road at Kubutambahan. Here at the road junction the village temple may be seen. The entrance, a tall *tjandi bentar* is of brick, rendered with lime mortar. The stone carving is elaborate and flowery in nature. The temple compound is unkempt. The only notable feature is on the eastern side where on an elevated platform protected in front by guardians, and flanked at each end by a *naga* balustrade, there are five small shrines, the wide, overhanging roofs of which are covered with corrugated iron, a feature common to nearly all temples in the north. There is also a *balé agung* or meeting place of open construction, rather long and narrow in plan in the Bali Aga fashion.

The town itself is dry and dusty in appearance and is typical of most towns in the area. The houses and shops are located on the street front. They are connected together to some extent by walls pierced by periodic gateways. These gateways, however, do not lead into individual family compounds, but are in effect the entrances to side streets or lanes along which the individual houses are located as individual units. This is a very noticeable feature here and at Bunkulan, Sangsit, Klontjing and Buleleng. In contrast to the south, the water buffalo is widely used as a beast of burden and high carts drawn by buffaloes are numerous in the streets.

Proceeding west from Kubutambahan the road passes a succession of rice fields and small towns. The walls of many of the houses and compounds in this area are made of volcanic pebbles and stones cemented together with lime mortar. At Bunkulan the *pura desa* has a deserted air and appears unused, but it is worth inspection because of the extraordinarily concentrated and lavish decorative carving on the 'split' outer gate, the pierced openings at intervals along the heavily-carved outer wall, and the *padu raksa* inner gate, similarly elaborately carved, with a three-tier pagoda-like roof topped by a symbolic crown. Similarly the *pura desa* of Sangsit is worth a brief visit to see the isolated *padu raksa* which originally formed the inner gate. This is 'rococo' in character, executed in a pinkish sandstone and is typical of the over-decorated work prevalent in these neglected temples of the north. There is, however, one very notable exception, the Pura Bedji at Sangsit.

## THE PURA BEDJI AT SANGSIT

The Pura Bedji is one of the most attractive and interesting temples in Bali. It is a large temple and is extremely ornate in its decoration and unusual in its layout and design. Yet strange to say, it is a *subak* temple, a temple dedicated to Dewi Sri, located on the edge of a coastal series of rice fields on the northern outskirts of the town of Sangsit. The whole temple is constructed in a fine sandstone with a slightly pink tinge. This stone happens to be somewhat subject to attrition by the elements and has become worn in many places. The whole structure, gates, walls and shrines, is almost completely covered on all surfaces with carved work comprising formalised flower and vine designs, *karang tjewiri*, pseudo-human forms, guardians, *garudas* and so on.

The outer gate is 'split', a *tjandi bentar*. It is set back from the road frontage in a carved, balustraded wall. The inner sanctuary area is served by a very wide *padu raksa* (Plate 45), the sill of which is elevated well above ground level and the door of which is approached by a unique three-sided series of ten stone steps rapidly decreasing in width as the door is reached. The top outline of this structure is decorated with a series of delicate, pierced, stone slabs suggestive of a series of stylised crowns. The inner sanctuary may be reached by small doors at ground level on either side. The reverse face of this *padu raksa* is equally fascinating. Like the front, it is completely covered with intricate carved designs, but in addition it has an attractive *aling aling* wall with a sweeping, curved balustrade on top.

The inner sanctuary is of unique design. The shrines are concentrated together at the south end of the sanctuary and form one integrated unit (Plate 46). There are, in effect, three main shrine areas. In the centre is a *gedong pesimpangan*, an enclosed shrine with carved stone walls, wooden doors and carved and gilded roof beams. To its left is a carved stone *padmasana* seat. To its right are two carved stone seats side by side also in the form of a *padmasana*, and a small shrine of more normal character. All these are set on a platform which rises from the ground in four successively receding tiers. Each shrine is approached from the front by a four-flight set of stone steps. At the level of the top of each tier, the steps leading to each of the shrines pass through a 'split' gate. The whole structure is again elaborately carved, the designs covering almost every available square foot of surface.

At the rear of the sanctuary is a small rectangular pond covered with water lilies. This is the bath for the gods, for this is a 'bath' temple. The sanctuary is beautified by the presence of a number of very large and very old frangipanni trees, whose shade and white blossoms lend enchantment to the scene. There is only one jarring note. The roof of the central shrine is covered in corrugated iron!

No visitor should miss this magnificent spectacle. To see it is alone justification for taking the long journey to northern Bali.

The port of Buleleng is an ordinary town with shopping and business areas somewhat 'Chinese' in character. The port itself is merely a reception area for merchandise arriving by sea. All ships, even the small inter-island sailing boats, must stand off the open and exposed beach and be unloaded by lighter. In the northwest monsoon the roadstead becomes untenable. Buleleng merges without a break into Singaradja, at the southern end of which is the former Governor's residence and buildings formerly occupied by government instrumentalities. Today they have a forlorn and forgotten air.

There is a library containing a stock of old Balinese *lontar* books, but this is seldom open to visitors.

From Singaradja the road to Denpasar leads southwards ascending the foothills to the village of Gitgit, after which it enters the heavily-forested mountain area, winding around the deeply-cut gullies and the prominent ridges until at a height of some 4,600 feet the summit of the road is reached. Here the country falls away sharply to the south and there is an excellent view down over Lake Bujan. To the right, obscured by the forest is the smaller Lake Tamblingan. To the left, in the distance, is the shimmering Lake Bratan. All three lie at an elevation of just over 4,000 feet in what may once have been an old volcanic crater. From the ridge above Lake Bujan the road descends steeply to the level of the lakes and continues south on level country to Tjandikuning, a village on the western shore of Lake Bratan.

LAKE BRATAN

The lake is of considerable extent, being almost square in shape and approximately two miles across. On the east the steep slopes of Mt. Tjatur are thickly forested right to the edge of the lake. To the west rise the majestic peaks of Mts. Pohen, Sengajang and Batukau, the last-named rising to an elevation of 7,707 feet. To the south the country falls away from the surface of the lake which seems almost to pour itself over the edge of the world into an invisible gulf below. In this magnificent and peaceful setting is the Pura Tjandikuning, a small, placid and somewhat isolated temple located right on the western edge of the lake. In fact it extends out into the lake itself. Entered by a 'split' gate, the single compound containing several simple thatched *balés* extends right to the water's edge. Here there are two delightful *merus* (Plate 47), one of eleven tiers located on a small promontory, and one to Dewi Sri, of three tiers, standing on a small island area in the lake itself. Thatched with black *idjuk*, these *merus* appear at their best and most ethereal on a day when the mountain mists descend over the lake blotting out all but the water and the shrines themselves.

The road passes by the southern end of the lake where there is a pleasant rest house at Bedugul. From there it descends the gradual slope of the southern lowlands passing through forest lands, rice terraces and a succession of villages. As has been mentioned in the last chapter, the mountain 'villages' are not true to pattern. The houses are individual, individually located and not formally associated in the normal walled village. This system extends southwards from the mountains for some distance and it is interesting to watch the gradual change in village structure from the individual houses as seen at Bedugul to the formal walled village with its contiguous walled family compounds typical of southern Balinese practice, which becomes completely re-established as the village of Luwus is reached some eight miles to the south of Budugul. From then on the scene is typical of the southern Balinese landscape as the road runs south through Mengwi and Kapal to Denpasar.

# 18

# *Klungkung, Tenganan and Karangasem*

Klungkung was formerly one of the most important seats of regional government in the early days of the Balinese kingdoms. The remains of the old palace (*puri*) of the Radja of Klungkung still exist, but are not maintained and the *puri* is not open to visitors. There is always an active market in the centre of Klungkung and traffic on the main road is diverted to enable it to function undisturbed. There are several notable antique shops. Beaten and embossed silverware is manufactured and to the north of the town there are a number of brickworks. The chief point of interest, however, is the old courthouse, the Kerta Gosa, which stands at the intersection of the main crossroads in the very centre of the town.

THE OLD COURTHOUSE—KERTA GOSA

The courthouse area was originally a part of the palace of the Dewa Agung of Klungkung and it consists of two structures. One of these is the courthouse itself (Plate 49). The other was originally used as a resting place for the judges of the court and as a place for them to hold private discussions concerning the cases before them and their judgements. The latter building is surrounded by a moat in brick and cut stone with the inevitable cover of water lily leaves. The building is approached from the main road through a *tjandi bentar*, across a short bridge over the moat and up two flights of steps which reach an elevated brick and stone platform surrounded by a pathway. A smaller carved masonry platform surmounts this and the whole is covered by a roof thatched with *idjuk*. The roof is supported by twelve timber posts around the periphery of the main platform and eight further pillars around the periphery of the inner platform. These pillars and the structure they support are carved and painted in gay and decorative colours. The underside of the roof is lined and covered with an extensive series of frescoes. This building is today used to display the *batiks*, wood carvings and other novelties sold there by women attracted to the site by the presence of so many tourists.

The courthouse itself is a smaller building of similar construction, located on the very corner of the main road intersection. It is approached by a short path from the main entrance which leads to a simple masonry platform with only a modest amount of decoration in the form of detailed carving. A short flight of nine steps gives access to the top of the platform where there is again a low subsidiary platform superimposed on it. Here the judges and the members of the Kerta sat in judgement, listened to the prosecution, heard pleadings and gave decisions. The judges were drawn from the Brahmana caste and were *pedandas*, or high priests. The members of the court sat on elaborately carved and gilded chairs around a table similarly decorated. These furnishings are displayed on the platform at the present time.

The platform on which the courthouse building stands is square in plan. The roof overhangs it slightly and is covered with a thatch of *idjuk*. The roof structure is elaborately carved and painted and is supported by twelve wooden pillars around the outside periphery of the main platform, and twelve wooden pillars around the periphery of the inner platform, undeniable evidence of the importance and standing of the building. Each post in the outer row of pillars is supported on the back of an animal carved in stone (Plate 49). This is a most interesting feature and is reminiscent of the same practice in Yucatan where the Mayas used the same architectural feature, known there as a 'chacmool'. The astonishing thing about the Kerta Gosa is the unusual variety of animals which form the bases of the pillars—elephants, lions, pigs, goats, lizards and so on. Be sure to inspect this most fascinating aspect.

The most notable feature, however, and that which seems predominantly to attract the visitor, is the roof. The carved, painted and gilded structure is lined and completely covered with frescoes. These take the form of a series of paintings which illustrate the penalties meted out in hell to sinners after they have departed from this mortal world. In particular the visitor should note the unpleasant fate which befalls the childless married woman, considered by the Balinese to be a sinner, and the dreadful nature of the emasculation which falls to the lot of the adulterer.

GELGEL

Just south of Klungkung towards the coast is the ancient town of Gelgel, the original pre-Madjapahit capital of the first King of Bali. Part of the village was destroyed in the 1963 eruption of Gunung Agung, the lava flow engulfing a number of houses and temple compounds. Here old brick gateways can be seen (Plate 48) half embedded in the lava which destroyed associated houses by setting fire to them. In the centre of the village is the original Royal Temple with a very large forecourt containing a long communal meeting house, a *balé agung* similar to those seen at Tenganan, and a very large *waringin* tree. Entrance to the outer court is by a large 'split' gate of unusual design. Normally the inside faces of a *tjandi bentar* are flat and unadorned. This gives the impression of a structure actually split down the centre after completion. The *tjandi bentar* at Gelgel (Plate 15) is very highly decorated with carved stone motifs on both the opposing faces of the gate.

The inner sanctuary is entered by a *padu raksa* of brick, and is most unusual in that its level is appreciably below that of the outer court. It contains several very large nine- and eleven-tiered *merus* which are amongst the largest in Bali and are supported on bases which are in some cases so slender as to appear quite inadequate.

A visit to Gelgel is well worth while. In addition to the old Royal Temple the visitor can see pottery making, carried on here as a cottage industry. The pots are thrown on very crude wooden potter's wheels rotated by hand, and are burnt in rice-straw fires by the roadside.

SAMPALAN AND GUNAKSA—VOLCANIC DESTRUCTION

Immediately to the east of Klungkung is the River Unda. Lava from the 1963 eruption of Mt. Agung flowed down the

L

valley of this river carrying away the bridge and isolating Karangasem and the east from road communication with Denpasar. A new bridge has only just been completed and opened (1969). In the next valley to the east an extensive lava flow completely destroyed the villages of Sampalan and Gunaksa, leaving nothing but an extensive lava plain whose bareness is today broken only by the remains of the village cemetery, its temple of the dead and associated *kepuh* tree. Here again, several isolated brick gateways in the former village precincts remain half buried in the lava as a grim reminder of the destruction caused by the 1963 eruption.

The main lava flow coming south down the side of Gunung Agung in the 1963 eruption was divided into two main streams by the coastal ranges of Bukit Sidemen. One flow followed the valleys to the west of the ranges and caused the damage seen in the Unda valley at Klungkung, at Gelgel and at the villages of Sampalan and Gunaksa. The other flow followed the valleys to the east of the ranges and engulfed a number of villages in the Karangasem area. Here they followed the valleys of the Rivers Buhu, Banka and Njuling, carrying away the bridge over the last-named river on the approach to Karangasem itself. In fact the two main towns of Klungkung and Karangasem themselves were extremely lucky to escape damage from these massive lava flows.

Between these two areas of destruction no damage was done because the coastal mountains protected the area from all lava activity. East of Gunaksa therefore the road to Karangasem passes for some miles along a narrow strip of land between the coastal ranges and the sea, which is still verdant and untouched. This portion of the southern coast of Bali is notable for its absence of rice fields and the predominance of coconut palms, bananas, cassava and tapioca. Here is the substantial fishing village of Kusamba where large numbers of the native outrigger sailing boats, *djukungs*, are to be seen drawn up on the black-sand beach. The fish is sold at open market under a large banyan tree on the main road nearby and from there is transported to the Denpasar market. In the morning the women can be seen on the roadside with heavy baskets of fresh fish on their heads, bringing them to market for sale.

THE BAT CAVE—GOA LAWAH

Immediately east of the village of Kusamba is the limestone cave of Goa Lawah. The entrance to the cave forms part of a shrine area or sanctuary, with shrines extending into the mouth of the cave itself. The cave is inhabited by some millions of bats which can be seen hanging in concentrated masses from the roof and walls. As is usual in such cases, the stench of bat guano is very pronounced. Numbers of large cockroaches scavenge amongst it. Sacred snakes can at times be seen resting on ledges within the cave which has become their home. On the seashore directly opposite the Bat Cave salt is harvested by solar evaporation of concentrated brine obtained from sea water.

A noticeable feature of this whole coastal area is the fact that the villages are no longer walled. The houses are of bamboo and thatch and are dispersed throughout the coconut groves and are not concentrated together in the form of formal villages. Not until Karangasem is reached is the normal walled compound type of village seen again. The walls in that area are constructed of lava boulders set in a matrix of lime mortar. The village of Bupbup is a characteristic example.

The coastal ranges terminate abruptly at an extensive lava flow in the valley of the River Buhu. A very fine view, both inland up the valley and south towards the sea, may be had from a roadside lookout at Sangiang, from which the road drops away steeply to the floor of the valley below. The road then traverses an extensive lava-devastated area until it reaches Karangasem four miles further on. Here the bridge approach over the River Njuling was destroyed in the 1963 eruptions and has only just been replaced (1969).

There is nothing of note to see in Karangasem itself, but beyond the town on the foreshore are the remains of the summer palace of the former Radja of Karangasem, known as the 'Water Palace' of Udjung. These were cut off from Karangasem for some time by lava flowing from Mt. Agung and have since been subject to great neglect. The palace buildings have seriously deteriorated, and are rapidly becoming derelict. The water which once surrounded the buildings, reflecting their beauty, no longer exists. Soy-bean crops are growing where former luxury prevailed. The 'Water Palace' is no longer worth visiting.

TENGANAN

At Senkidu on the main Klungkung-Karangasem road, a shady and secluded track leads north for three miles to the village of Pasedahan. At the far end of this village the road stops. Further progress can only be made on foot. Here lies the ancient Bali Aga village of Tenganan. It is entered by a flight of stone steps leading to a small gate in the wall which surrounds the whole village. Once inside the village compound the visitor will immediately note its entirely different and impersonal character and feel the sense of quiet, solitude and remoteness that prevails.

The village is essentially built around a central concourse (Plate 50) running north and south. This concourse is wide and well-grassed, and rises in successive terraces as it moves uphill to the north. Sloping stone ramps reach from terrace to terrace. Along each side of the concourse are the house compounds, each within its own individual wall. Each has its own entrance gateway fitted with a single-leaf, wooden door. Each compound is more or less identical in layout and is as shown in Fig. 7.

The entrance gate leads into the courtyard. Immediately inside it is a small shrine (A), dedicated to the spirits of the King and the ancestors of the occupants. This is called the *Sanggah Pesimpangan*. Built against the front wall of the compound is the *balé sutji* (B), a pavilion used for the preparation of offerings and for receiving visitors. Because the thatched roof of this *balé* can be seen above the front wall of the compound, the appearance from the street is as of a house directly entered by a front door, and a continuous row of these houses as is seen at Tenganan on each side of the central concourse, looks very much like a terrace of single-storey houses in a western style town (Plate 50). Alongside the *balé sutji* is a second shrine (C), the *Sanggah Kemulan*, dedicated to the *trimurti*, or the trinity of gods, Siwa, Wisnu and Brahma. The rice granary (D), is elevated on posts and the space underneath it is generally used as the family living and sleeping quarters, *djineng*. Behind it is the *paon*, or

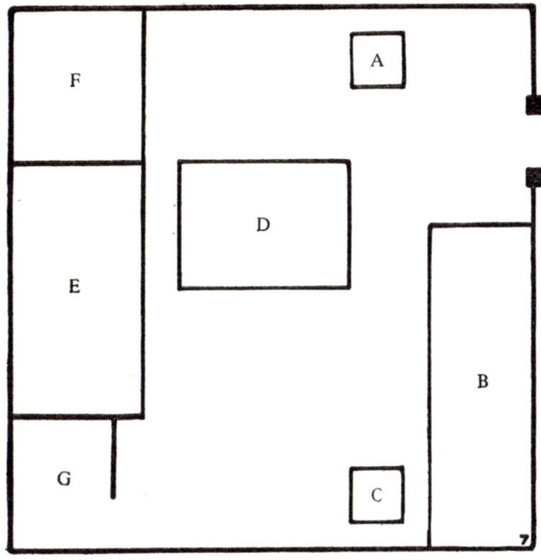

7. Typical family compound at Tenganan. A, *Sanggah pesimpangan,* or shrine to the king. B, *Balé sutji,* a formal pavilion. C, *Sanggah kemulan,* or shrine to the trinity. D, *Djineng,* rice granary with living quarters under it. E, *Paon,* or kitchen. F, Pigsty. G, Bath and toilet.

kitchen (E) and next to it the pigsty (F). In one corner is the bath and toilet area (G), an unroofed, open space. The walls of the compound are constructed of volcanic stone boulders in a matrix of mud or lime mortar.

At intervals along the wide central concourse are four long meeting houses with raised, platform-type floors. These are known as *balé agung,* and are used by the sectional village councils for official discussions and group meetings. At the far end of the village is a larger meeting place, the *balé paruman desa,* which is the central meeting house for the village as a whole and serves also as the venue for drama and dancing and village festivals. Between the successive *balé agung* are communal rice granaries and some minor buildings. A central *kulkul* serves to summon the villagers to meetings and other village functions.

Tenganan is probably the sole remaining village in Bali today in which a completely communal society still exists. The village itself, the rice fields attached to it and the property belonging to it are all owned by the whole community and all villagers have an equity in the total wealth of the community. The village is in fact a land-owner of considerable size and power, and by collecting rent from working tenants in the form of rice and other products, has become wealthy. As a consequence the villagers themselves do little or no menial work and are able to devote a great deal of time to other pursuits. Many of them are skilled weavers and earn extra income by this means. In fact the village of Tenganan is noted for the unique production of a type of woven cloth known as *grinsing*. The patterned cloth is produced by the *ikat* method, the unusual feature being that in this case both the warp and the weft are preassembled, the pattern outlined in each by wrapping the yarn with fibres, and fixed by dyeing. Subsequent assembly on the loom is such as to reproduce the required pattern with a characteristic vagueness of outline which has distinct attraction. Because of the involved method of manufacture, true *grinsing* cloth is very expensive. Its production is undertaken only at certain propitious times.

The village of Tenganan is notable for the almost complete absence of village temples. The *pura desa* will be found just inside the main entrance at the south end and is comprised of several simple shrines thatched with *idjuk* and surrounded by a wild profusion of frangipanni trees. The original gates of the village are located at the north and south ends of the concourse.

Because of its completely different character and atmosphere as compared to the ordinary Balinese village, Tenganan must be seen by any visitor who is in any way interested in the history and development of the Balinese community.

# 19

## *Bukit Djambul and Besakih*

North from Klungkung the road to Rendang rises gradually through a long succession of rice terraces. It first follows the valley of the River Unda and then the valley of the River Telagawadja until four miles out of Klungkung it sweeps up the steep hillside at Bukit Djambul and climbs out of the valley to run along the higher ridge country. Here the *sawahs* rise from the bottom of the valley, terrace after terrace after terrace, in an endless succession of steps, until they reach the very tops of the hills some 1,500 feet above. The views from the road are simply magnificent. Nowhere else could one see such a spectacular development of terraces. Only the Balinese could have developed a system of irrigation capable of meeting the requirements of the *sawahs* on such a steep slope and over such a seemingly endless cascade. From the village of Pesaban at the top of the ridge the view over the valley and the narrow coastal plain to the sea beyond is an exquisite vista of subtly blended greens. The rice terraces of Bukit Djambul must be seen by every visitor. But then, of course, so must the 'Mother Temple' at Besakih, and they are on the same road.

After ascending the hillside the road continues through a succession of smaller rice terraces and quiet mountain villages as it follows the course of the valley of the upper River Djinah. Three miles further on it reaches the village of Rendang. This is a quiet and pleasant village of mud walls and grass thatch, somewhat disorderly in appearance, but for that reason perhaps more attractive. Here the villagers seem to go about their daily tasks with quiet and happy energy, drying sweet potato in the sun by the roadside, pounding rice, fetching water from the fast flowing channels which run submerged in the grassy verge at the roadside, or bathing in them.

From Rendang the road climbs in a northeasterly direction straight up the flank of the great volcanic cone of the sacred mountain, Gunung Agung. As the road rises, verdure is left behind. Vegetation becomes stunted and scrubby. The mountain ahead rises barren from the landscape covered in its pale purple mantle of lava. On a clear day the sight is an unforgettable one, when five miles above Rendang the visitor is suddenly confronted with the magnificent spectacle of the 'Mother Temple' of Besakih (Plate 51), with its majestic sequence of terraced courts and staircases, and its multitude of tall *merus* outlined as a black silhouette against the background of the mountain.

The 'Mother Temple' at Besakih is the oldest and most sacred temple on the island. Its exact age is uncertain but legend has it that the original core was erected in the second century by the seer Sri Maharkadia who was the first to teach Siwa Hinduism in the island and who gave the name 'Bali' to it. The 'Mother Temple' provides precincts for all Hindu sects and for each of the original Balinese States. Each of the Radjas and their courts formerly made annual pilgrimage to the temple. It is the seat of the godly spirits of the holy seers and the respected kings and ancestors of the Balinese people. It is the largest temple in Bali. It is a temple of great complexity and yet at the same time a temple of appealing simplicity. It is unique.

There are actually three temple areas involved at Besakih. The main central section is by far the most extensive and is known as the Pura Panataran Agung. This simply means the 'greatest temple of all the people'. To its west, separated from it by one of the many ravines running down the mountainside is the Balu Badek. To its east, separated from it by still another ravine, is the Kidul. These are minor elements, seldom visited. We will confine our attention to the Pura Panataran Agung alone.

The Pura Panataran consists of six walled courts, one behind the other, increasing in elevation from the front of the temple to the rear as they ascend the steep slope of the mountainside. From the *wantilan* at the end of the road, a stepped pathway leads upwards past the first temple compound to be established on the site. This is in a small walled courtyard entered by a simple undecorated 'split' gate and consists essentially of one ancient seven-tiered *meru* thatched with *idjuk*.

This path leads to a wide level area of ground at the foot of the majestic front aspect of the temple forming the southern wall of the first court. This rises in seven levels, each carrying six guardians, three on either side of the wide central staircase whose forty-nine steep steps lead to a *tjandi bentar* which affords entry to the first court. This 'split' gate is one of great simplicity and is guarded by two *raksasas*. The outer court is intended for festival activities and is provided with simple pavilions for the preparation of offerings and to provide platforms for orchestras and for other players. One of these, with a stone base, is placed right behind the split gate, obstructing its opening, and acts, no doubt, as an *aling aling* wall.

The second court, also a very large area, is entered by a *padu raksa* guarded by a pair of lions, and approached by a flight of twenty-one steps. The *padu raksa* is again, although of stone, unadorned except for a simple seven-tiered pagoda-like roof design and the usual *karang tjewiri* over the doorway. It is this very simplicity which gives emphasis to the size and majesty of Besakih. The second court incorporates further pavilions for the preparation of offerings, but in addition houses the great *padmasana* of the temple. This is a shrine intended for the trinity of gods, Siwa, Wisnu and Brahma. It is a comparatively modern addition to the original temple. It consists of a wide stone platform reached by a central stone staircase with carved *naga* balustrades. On the platform, side by side, backs to the mountain, are three separate, carved-stone chairs. They are remarkable for their unusual design. Each chair, standing on its own pedestal base, has a high straight back, in outline reminiscent of a Hindu 'prang', surmounted by a crown and with a *garuda* carved on the back. The *padmasana* is well worth careful inspection in detail. Note also the one, very large, eleven-tiered *meru* of simple timber construction, to the left of the steps leading to the third court.

The third court is reached by a flight of twenty-four steps. There is no gate. The remaining three courts are smaller and the differences in level between them are not so great. They are reached successively by simple flights of stone steps. Each of them contains a number of *merus*. It is the large number of *merus*, of simple but varied design in timber, thatched with black *idjuk* fibre, which gives the 'Mother Temple' its unusual character. It is the contrast between their black silhouettes and either the view back over the coastal plain to the sea, or the view upwards to the shimmering purple-brown lava-fields of the mountain, that makes the scene so attractive. Here will be seen *merus* of all types, with from three to eleven roofs, small and large alike. Some are tall and narrow. Others are short and wide. Some appear more like pavilions with three-tiered roofs. Others are wide at the base, curving inwards and upwards to finish in a tall slender spire.

Adjoining the main temple on the eastern side are several walled sanctuary areas, small in size but varied in interest. As is the 'Mother Temple' itself, these sanctuaries are occupied in the main by *merus*, with a small number of pavilions which, like the houses of the high, mountain villages, are covered with split-bamboo tiles. The *merus* are thatched with *idjuk* except for a series in a sanctuary known as the 'Kings' Area', in which the *merus* are unique. They are constructed in brick and the tiered roofs are rendered in lime mortar (Plate 52). In this sanctuary there is also a small shrine with a stone base on each of the corners of which a *karang tjuring*, or stylised *garuda* has been carved. These figures are particularly interesting as representing an early form in the development of this motif. These small subsidiary sanctuaries are separated from the main temple by a narrow lane which returns to the platform in front of the main temple entrance.

A last look at the 'Mother Temple' will be rewarding. From the approach road it appears to tower above the landscape. The upper terraces are largely hidden from view. Vertical perspective draws the eye inevitably from the base up the rise of the magnificent staircase to the points of the 'split' gate above and on to the distant summit of the azure mountain beyond. The jet-black *merus* dissect the skyline like magic symbols of a supreme peace. Unforgettable!

# Bibliography

Those interested in studying the Island of Bali, its people and their customs in greater detail will find the following short list of published works on the subject informative and interesting.


Belo, Jane: 'A Study of a Balinese Family', *The American Anthropologist*, Vol. 38, No. 1, 1936.

Covarrubias, Miguel: *Island of Bali*. Cassell, London, 1937.

Faber, G. H. von: *Bali, Land of a Thousand Temples*. H. van Ingen, Sourabaya, 1938.

Mathews, Anna: *The Night of Purnama*.

McKie, Ronald and Bernay, Beryl: *Bali*. Angus and Robertson, Sydney, 1969.

Raffles, Sir Stamford: *The History of Java*. London, 1830.

Spies, Walter and de Zoete, Beryl: *Dance and Drama in Bali*. Faber and Faber, London, 1938.

Zainuddin, Ailsa: *A Short History of Indonesia*. Cassell Australia, Melbourne, 1968.

# Index